HEALTHY NINJA CREAMi

PROTEIN COOKBOOK

Simple & Mouthwatering Homemade Frozen Treats| Smoothie Bowl, Ice
Cream, Sorbet, Gelato, Milkshake Recipes for Beginners and Advance Users

Caroline Eve RDN

Copyright

CONTENTS

INTRODUCTION 4

OVERVIEW OF THE NINJA CREAMI 5

BENEFITS OF PROTEIN-PACKED RECIPES 7

TIPS FOR USING THE NINJA CREAMI 9

PROTEIN-INFUSED SMOOTHIE BOWL 11

ICE CREAM WITH ADDED PROTEIN 25

PROTEIN MILKSHAKES 42

SORBET ENRICHED WITH PROTEIN 55

GELATO WITH ADDED PROTEIN 66

ACKNOWLEDGMENTS 76

MEASUREMENTS CHARTS

RECIPES INDEX

Introduction

As I embarked on my journey to embrace a healthier lifestyle, I found myself exploring the world of protein-rich cooking with the trusty companion, the Ninja Creami. It wasn't always an easy path – there were moments of trial and error, some culinary mishaps, but also plenty of satisfying victories. The decision to prioritize protein in my meals wasn't just about a fleeting fitness trend; it was a conscious choice to fuel my body with the nutrients it needed.

In the midst of experimenting with various protein-packed recipes, the idea for this cookbook was born. I realized that there's a shared desire among many to infuse their diets with more protein, yet the process can seem overwhelming or, at times, monotonous. The Ninja Creami became my kitchen ally, transforming ordinary meals into protein-rich delights that were not only nutritious but also delicious.

This cookbook is a culmination of my personal experiences – the flavors that worked, the unexpected combinations that surprised, and the joy of discovering how simple it can be to elevate everyday dishes. I'm not a professional chef, just someone who appreciates good food that nourishes the body. Through this collection of recipes, I aim to demystify the process of integrating protein into daily meals using the versatile Ninja Creami.

So, join me on this practical and flavorful journey. Let's make protein-packed cooking accessible, enjoyable, and a seamless part of our lives. Whether you're a fitness enthusiast, a busy parent, or simply someone seeking wholesome meals without sacrificing taste, this cookbook is crafted with you in mind. Here's to embracing a protein-enriched lifestyle with the help of the Ninja Creami!

Equipped with your new Ninja Creamy, welcome to the thrilling world of culinary creativity! Before diving into the vast array of protein-packed recipes, let's ensure a smooth start with some basic guidelines.

Open and Configure your Machine

❖ Open Your Ninja Creamy Box: Carefully unpack your Ninja Creamy and inspect all components. Ensure that nothing is damaged or missing. Your package should typically include the base unit, blending pitcher, single-serve cups, and accompanying lids.

❖ Review the Manual: Inside the box, you'll find a comprehensive manual that serves as your go-to guide for operating and maintaining the Ninja Creamy. Take a moment to read through the manual, familiarizing yourself with the features, safety precautions, and cleaning instructions.

Assemble Your Ninja Creami Together

❖ Base Unit Setup: Place the Ninja Creamy base unit on a clean, flat surface. Ensure it is securely positioned before starting any blending operations.

❖ Blending Pitcher Assembly: Attach the blending pitcher to the base unit by aligning the arrows on both components. The pitcher should click into place, indicating a secure connection.

❖ Single-Serve Cup Setup: If using the single-serve cups, attach the blending blade assembly to the cup before securing it onto the base unit. Ensure a tight connection to prevent any leaks during blending.

Turn on Basic Function

❖ Plug in Your Ninja Creamy: Attach the power cord to an appropriate wall outlet. Make sure the power switch on the base unit is in the "OFF" position before plugging it in.

❖ Safety Interlock: The Ninja Creamy is equipped with a safety interlock system. The unit will not operate unless the pitcher or single-serve cup is correctly assembled onto the base unit.

❖ Control Panel: Familiarize yourself with the control panel. Depending on your model, it may include buttons for power, speed settings, and pulse functionality. Refer to the manual for specific details on each control.

Exploring Pre-Programmed Settings

❖ Check for Pre-Programmed Settings: Some Ninja Creamy models come with pre-programmed settings tailored for specific recipes. Review your manual to understand these settings and how they can simplify your blending experience.

❖ Adjusting Speeds and Pulse: Experiment with the variable speed settings and pulse function to achieve the desired texture for your recipes. The versatility of the Ninja Creamy allows for precise control over blending.

Cleaning and Maintenance

❖ Refer to the Cleaning Instructions: The manual provides detailed instructions on how to clean each component of the Ninja Creamy. Follow these guidelines to maintain hygiene and ensure the longevity of your appliance.

❖ Store Components Properly: When not in use, store the blending pitcher, single-serve cups, and blades in a clean and dry area. Proper storage helps prevent damage and ensures that your Ninja Creamy is ready for the next culinary adventure.

The manual inside the box is your ultimate companion on this culinary journey. It contains valuable information to make the most out of your Ninja Creamy. Now, let's unleash the full potential of this powerful appliance and start blending delicious protein-packed creations!

Protein-packed recipes offer a myriad of benefits that extend beyond merely satisfying hunger. Incorporating ample protein into your meals contributes to overall well-being and can positively impact various aspects of your health. Here are some key benefits of embracing protein-rich culinary choices:

❖ Muscle Maintenance and Growth: Protein is essential for the maintenance and repair of tissues, making it a fundamental building block for muscles. Protein-packed recipes provide the necessary amino acids that support muscle growth and recovery, making them particularly beneficial for individuals engaged in physical activities or those aiming to build and maintain muscle mass.

❖ Satiety and Weight Management: Including protein in your meals enhances the feeling of fullness and satiety. This can be advantageous for those striving to manage their weight, as it helps curb unnecessary snacking and promotes better control over calorie intake. Protein-packed recipes contribute to a more satisfying and sustained sense of fullness.

❖ Metabolism Boost: The thermic effect of food (TEF) refers to the energy expended during the digestion and absorption of nutrients. Protein has a higher TEF compared to fats and carbohydrates, meaning that the body burns more calories in the process of metabolizing protein. Including protein in recipes can contribute to a modest boost in metabolism.

❖ Blood Sugar Regulation: Protein has a stabilizing effect on blood sugar levels. When combined with carbohydrates, it can slow down the absorption of sugars, preventing rapid spikes and crashes in blood glucose. This can be particularly beneficial for individuals with diabetes or those aiming to maintain consistent energy levels throughout the day.

❖ Improved Body Composition: Protein-packed recipes play a role in promoting a healthy body composition by supporting fat loss while preserving lean muscle mass. This is vital for achieving a balanced and sustainable approach to weight management.

❖ Enhanced Nutrient Absorption: Protein aids in the absorption of essential nutrients, ensuring that the body effectively utilizes vitamins and minerals present in the diet.

This synergy contributes to overall nutritional efficiency and supports various bodily functions.

❖ Wound Healing and Immune Support: Proteins are integral to the body's immune system and play a crucial role in wound healing. Protein-packed recipes provide the necessary nutrients for a robust immune response and expedited recovery from injuries or illnesses.

❖ Long-lasting Energy: Unlike simple carbohydrates that provide quick but short-lived energy, protein offers sustained energy. Protein-packed recipes can help maintain energy levels over an extended period, making them ideal choices for busy lifestyles.

The benefits of incorporating protein-packed recipes into your diet extend beyond taste and culinary satisfaction. These recipes contribute to overall health, supporting muscle function, weight management, and various physiological processes essential for a vibrant and energetic lifestyle.

Tips for Using the Ninja Creami

1. Prep Ingredients in Advance: Before using the Ninja Creamy, ensure that your ingredients are washed, chopped, and ready to go. This streamlines the blending process and ensures a smoother texture in your final protein-packed creations.

2. Use Frozen Ingredients for Creaminess: For an extra creamy texture, consider using frozen fruits, vegetables, or even yogurt cubes. This not only adds a refreshing chill to your recipes but also enhances the creaminess without the need for additional ice.

3. Balance Liquid and Solid Ingredients: Achieve the perfect consistency by balancing liquid and solid ingredients. Start with the recommended liquid base, gradually adding solids to avoid overwhelming the blades. This approach ensures efficient blending and prevents any strain on the Ninja Creamy.

4. Layer Ingredients Strategically: When preparing smoothies or shakes, layering ingredients strategically can prevent clumping and promote even blending. Place softer items closer to the blades and denser ingredients towards the top for optimal results.

5. Experiment with Protein Sources: Don't limit yourself to one protein source. Experiment with a variety of proteins such as whey, plant-based, or Greek yogurt to discover unique flavors and nutritional profiles. This adds diversity to your protein-packed recipes.

6. Customize Texture with Ice or Liquid: Adjust the texture of your recipes by controlling the amount of ice or liquid added. For a thicker consistency, use less liquid or more frozen ingredients. If a thinner texture is preferred, increase the liquid content.

7. Pulse for Precision: When fine-tuning the texture of your recipes, utilize the pulse function on the Ninja Creamy. This allows for precise control over blending, helping you achieve the desired consistency without over-processing.

8. Clean Immediately After Use: To maintain the longevity of your Ninja Creamy and ensure the next blending session is hassle-free, clean the appliance immediately after use. This prevents residues from hardening and makes cleanup a quick and easy task.

9. Experiment with Flavor Enhancers: Elevate the taste of your protein-packed creations by experimenting with flavor enhancers. Add a dash of cinnamon, a hint of vanilla extract, or a spoonful of nut butter to infuse exciting flavors into your recipes.

10. Monitor Texture During Blending: Keep an eye on the blending process and pause occasionally to check the texture. This allows you to make real-time adjustments, ensuring that your protein-packed recipes meet your desired consistency.

11. Utilize Single-Serve Cups for Convenience: Take advantage of the single-serve cups for quick and convenient protein shakes. These cups are not only portable but also simplify portion control, making them ideal for on-the-go nutrition.

Using these tips into your Ninja Creamy routine will not only enhance the efficiency of your blending but also open up a world of possibilities for crafting delicious and nutritious protein-packed recipes.

PROTEIN-INFUSED SMOOTHIE BOWL

Tropical Sunrise Bowl

Wake up to the vibrant flavors of a Tropical Sunrise Bowl. Packed with protein and tropical goodness, this bowl combines exotic fruits and a luscious base to create a refreshing and energizing breakfast.

Prep Time: 15 minutes| Serves: 2 servings

Ingredients

2 frozen bananas

1 cup frozen mango chunks

1 cup frozen pineapple chunks

2 scoops vanilla or tropical-flavored protein powder

1/2 cup coconut milk

Toppings: Fresh berries, sliced kiwi, shredded coconut, chia seeds

Nutritional Information (Per Serving): Calories: 280| Total Fat: 8g| Saturated Fat: 5g| Cholesterol: 5mg| Protein: 20g| Sodium: 30mg| Carbohydrates: 40g| Dietary Fiber: 6g| Sugar: 22g

Hints and Tactics

You can add more or less coconut milk to change the thickness. To enhance the texture, you can add a layer of granola on top as a crunchy topping.

Directions

1. In the Ninja Creami blending pitcher, combine frozen bananas, frozen mango chunks, frozen pineapple chunks, protein powder, and coconut milk.

2. Secure the blending pitcher onto the Ninja Creami base and blend on medium speed until the mixture is smooth and creamy.

3. Transfer the tropical mixture to bowls.

4. Top with fresh berries, sliced kiwi, shredded coconut, and chia seeds.

5. Serve immediately and enjoy the Tropical Sunrise Bowl.

Green Power Protein Smoothie

Fuel your day with the nutrient-packed goodness of the Green Power Protein Smoothie. This vibrant and protein-rich blend of greens, fruits, and protein powder is a perfect way to kick-start your morning or replenish your energy after a workout.

Prep Time: 7 minutes| Serves: 2 servings

Ingredients

2 cups fresh spinach leaves

1 cup kale leaves, stems removed

1 banana, peeled and frozen

1/2 cucumber, peeled and sliced

1/2 avocado, peeled and pitted

1 scoop plant-based protein powder (vanilla or unflavored)

1 tablespoon chia seeds

1 cup coconut water

Ice cubes (optional)

Nutritional Information (Per Serving): Calories: 250| Fat: 5g| Saturated Fat: 1g| Cholesterol: 10mg| Protein: 20g| Sodium: 80mg| Carbohydrates: 40g| Dietary Fiber: 7g| Sugar: 20g

Hints and Tactics

For variation, try experimenting with other greens like Swiss chard or kale. To enhance the texture, you can garnish with a sprinkle of chia seeds on top.

Directions

1. In the Ninja Creami blending pitcher, combine fresh spinach leaves, kale leaves, frozen banana, sliced cucumber, avocado, plant-based protein powder, chia seeds, and coconut water.

2. Blend the ingredients until the smoothie reaches a creamy consistency.

3. If a colder smoothie is desired, add ice cubes and blend again until well incorporated.

4. Pour the Green Power Protein Smoothie into glasses.

5. Garnish with a sprinkle of chia seeds or a slice of cucumber if desired.

6. Serve immediately and enjoy the invigorating taste of green power.

Unleash the power of greens with the Green Hulk Smoothie, a refreshing and nutrient-packed beverage that combines the strength of spinach, the sweetness of kiwi, and the protein boost from Greek yogurt. This smoothie is a green powerhouse to invigorate your day.

Prep Time: 7 minutes| Serves:| 2 servings

Ingredients

2 cups fresh spinach

2 kiwis, peeled and sliced

1/2 cucumber, peeled and sliced

1/2 avocado, peeled and pitted

1/2 cup Greek yogurt

1 tablespoon honey

1 cup water or coconut water

Ice cubes (optional)

Nutritional Information (Per Serving): Calories: 280| Fat: 12g| Saturated Fat: 2g| Cholesterol: 10mg| Protein: 15g| Sodium: 60mg| Carbohydrates: 35g| Dietary Fiber: 10g| Sugar: 20g

Directions

1. In the Ninja Creami blending pitcher, combine fresh spinach, kiwis, cucumber, avocado, Greek yogurt, honey, and water (or coconut water).

2. Blend on high speed until the smoothie reaches a silky and well-blended consistency.

3. If desired, add ice cubes and blend again for a colder texture.

4. Pour into glasses and embrace the strength of the Green Hulk Smoothie

Hints and Tactics

Modify the thickness by changing the quantity of liquid. For a final flourish, place a kiwi slice on the edge of the glass as a garnish.

Experience a burst of tropical vibrancy with the Pinktastic Pitaya Smoothie. This delightful blend showcases the exotic and nutrient-rich pitaya (dragon fruit) along with a medley of refreshing fruits, creating a visually stunning and health-packed smoothie.

Prep Time: 5 minutes| Serves: 2 servings

Ingredients

1 cup frozen pitaya chunks

1 cup frozen strawberries

1 ripe banana

1/2 cup Greek yogurt

1 tablespoon honey

1 cup coconut water

Ice cubes (optional)

Nutritional Information (Per Serving): Calories: 180| Fat: 2g| Saturated Fat: 1g| Cholesterol: 5mg| Protein: 5g| Sodium: 60mg| Carbohydrates: 40g| Dietary Fiber: 5g| Sugar: 25g

Hints and Tactics

Try varying the flavor profiles by experimenting with other frozen berries. Modify the amount of honey according to your choice.

Directions

1. In the Ninja Creami blending pitcher, combine frozen pitaya chunks, frozen strawberries, ripe banana, Greek yogurt, honey, and coconut water.

2. Blend on high speed until the smoothie reaches a vibrant and smooth consistency.

3. If desired, add ice cubes and blend again for a colder texture.

4. Pour into glasses and relish the Pinktastic Pitaya Smoothie.

Sweet Potato Pie Spice Protein Smoothie

Experience the comforting flavors of fall with the Sweet Potato Pie Spice Protein Smoothie. This protein-packed blend combines the goodness of sweet potato with warm spices, creating a smoothie that's not only delicious but also nourishing and satisfying.

Prep Time: 8 minutes| Serves: 2 servings

Ingredients

1 cup cooked and cooled sweet potato, mashed

1 banana

1 cup almond milk

1 scoop vanilla protein powder

1/2 teaspoon ground cinnamon

1/4 teaspoon ground nutmeg

1 tablespoon maple syrup

1 cup ice cubes

Nutritional Information (Per Serving): Calories: 220| Total Fat: 3g| Saturated Fat: 0.5g| Cholesterol: 15mg| Protein: 15g| Sodium: 120mg| Carbohydrates: 35g| Dietary Fiber: 5g| Sugar: 18g

Hints and Tactics

Ensure the sweet potato is thoroughly cooked and cooled before blending. Add a dash of cinnamon as a finishing touch.

Direction

1. In the Ninja Creami blending pitcher, combine mashed sweet potato, banana, almond milk, vanilla protein powder, ground cinnamon, ground nutmeg, and maple syrup.

2. Secure the blending pitcher onto the Ninja Creami base and blend on medium speed until the mixture is smooth.

3. Add ice cubes and blend again until the smoothie reaches a creamy and chilled consistency.

4. Pour into glasses and enjoy the wholesome goodness of the Sweet Potato Pie Spice Protein Smoothie.

Elevate your energy levels and embrace a burst of vibrant nutrients with the Spirulina Smoothie Sunshine. Packed with the goodness of spirulina, this refreshing and nutrient-rich smoothie is a delightful way to start your day with a boost of vitality.

Prep Time: 5 minutes| Serves: 2 servings

Ingredients

1 banana

1 cup pineapple chunks (fresh or frozen)

1 tablespoon spirulina powder

1/2 cup Greek yogurt

1 tablespoon honey

1 cup coconut water

Ice cubes (optional)

Nutritional Information (Per Serving): Calories: 180| Total Fat: 2g| Saturated Fat: 1g| Cholesterol: 5mg| Protein: 6g| Sodium: 70mg| Carbohydrates: 35g| Dietary Fiber: 3g| Sugar: 22g

Hints and Tactics

Try adding some fresh spinach for an added nutritional boost. Add a pineapple slice as a garnish to give it a tropical flair.

Direction

1. In the Ninja Creami blending pitcher, combine banana, pineapple chunks, spirulina powder, Greek yogurt, honey, and coconut water.

2. Secure the blending pitcher onto the Ninja Creami base and blend on medium speed until the mixture is smooth.

3. If desired, add ice cubes and blend again for a cooler texture.

4. Pour into glasses and bask in the invigorating Spirulina Smoothie Sunshine.

Satisfy your sweet cravings with the Strawberry Shortcake Smoothie, a delightful blend that captures the essence of the classic dessert. This protein-packed smoothie combines the sweetness of strawberries with the richness of vanilla, creating a guilt-free treat.

Prep Time: 5 minutes | Serves: 2 servings

Ingredients

2 cups fresh strawberries, hulled

1 cup vanilla Greek yogurt

1 cup almond milk

1/2 cup rolled oats

1 tablespoon honey

1 teaspoon vanilla extract

1 cup ice cubes

Nutritional Information (Per Serving): Calories: 200| Total Fat: 3g| Saturated Fat: 1g| Cholesterol: 10mg| Protein: 10g| Sodium: 50mg| Carbohydrates: 35g| Dietary Fiber: 5g| Sugar: 18g

Direction

1. In the Ninja Creami blending pitcher, combine fresh strawberries, vanilla Greek yogurt, almond milk, rolled oats, honey, and vanilla extract.

2. Secure the blending pitcher onto the Ninja Creami base and blend on medium speed until the mixture is smooth.

3. Add ice cubes and blend again until the smoothie reaches a creamy and chilled consistency.

4. Pour into glasses and indulge in the guilt-free Strawberry Shortcake Smoothie.

Hints and Tactics

❖ Add a touch of crushed graham crackers as a garnish for a shortcake-inspired finish.

❖ Enhance creaminess by opting for frozen strawberries.

Savor the delightful layers of goodness in the Greek Yogurt Berry Parfait with Protein Granola. This protein-packed parfait combines the tanginess of Greek yogurt with the sweetness of berries and the crunch of protein granola for a wholesome and satisfying treat.

Prep Time: 10 minutes| Assembly Time: 5 minutes| Serves: 2 servings

Ingredients

For Protein Granola

1 cup old-fashioned oats

1/4 cup almonds, chopped

1/4 cup walnuts, chopped

1/4 cup pumpkin seeds

1/4 cup honey or maple syrup

1 tablespoon coconut oil, melted

1 scoop vanilla protein powder

1/2 teaspoon vanilla extract

Pinch of salt

For Parfait

2 cups Greek yogurt (full-fat or low-fat)

1 cup mixed berries (strawberries, blueberries, raspberries)

Honey for drizzling (optional)

Nutritional Information (Per Serving): Calories: 400 Total Fat: 20g Saturated Fat: 4g Cholesterol: 10mg Protein: 25g Sodium: 100mg Carbohydrates: 40g Dietary Fiber: 6g Sugar: 20g

Direction

For Protein Granola

1. Preheat the Ninja Creami using the "Bake" function.
2. In a bowl, mix together oats, almonds, walnuts, pumpkin seeds, honey (or maple syrup), melted coconut oil, vanilla protein powder, vanilla extract, and a pinch of salt.
3. Spread the mixture on the Ninja Creami baking tray.
4. Bake in the preheated Ninja Creami for 15-20 minutes or until golden brown, stirring halfway through.
5. Allow the protein granola to cool completely before breaking it into clusters.

For Parfait

6. In serving glasses or bowls, layer Greek yogurt, mixed berries, and protein granola clusters.
7. Layers should be repeated until the glasses are full.
8. Drizzle honey on top if desired.
9. Serve immediately and relish the delightful combination of creamy yogurt, sweet berries, and crunchy protein granola.

Hints and Tactics

Make a larger batch of protein granola and store it in an airtight container for future use.

Alter the sweetness by varying the amount of honey or choosing flavored Greek yogurt.

Experience the perfect marriage of coffee and protein with the Mocha Protein Affogato. This indulgent treat combines the bold flavors of espresso with the richness of chocolate protein, creating a delightful and protein-packed dessert or energizing pick-me-up.

Prep Time: 5 minutes| Serves: 2 servings

Ingredients

2 shots of espresso or 1/2 cup strong brewed coffee

2 scoops chocolate protein powder

1/2 cup vanilla almond milk (or your choice of milk)

2 small scoops vanilla or coffee-flavored ice cream

Nutritional Information (Per Serving): Calories: 180| Total Fat: 6g| Saturated Fat: 2g| Cholesterol: 20mg| Protein: 15g| Sodium: 70mg| Carbohydrates: 15g| Dietary Fiber: 2g| Sugar: 8g

Hints and Tactics

Experiment with different protein powder flavors to introduce some variety. Optionally, enhance the dish by garnishing it with a dusting of cocoa powder or chocolate shavings.

Direction

1. Brew the espresso or strong coffee.
2. In the Ninja Creami blending pitcher, combine the hot espresso or coffee with chocolate protein powder. Stir until the protein powder is fully dissolved.
3. Pour the mocha protein mixture evenly into two espresso cups or small glasses.
4. Add a scoop of vanilla or coffee-flavored ice cream to each cup.
5. Serve immediately and enjoy the creamy and protein-enriched Mocha Protein Affogato.

Embrace the warmth and health benefits of turmeric with the Golden Milk Smoothie. This nourishing and spiced blend combines turmeric with banana and coconut, creating a golden-hued smoothie that's both soothing and nutritious.

Prep Time: 7 minutes| Serves: 2 servings

Ingredients

1 large banana

1 cup coconut milk

1 teaspoon turmeric powder

1/2 teaspoon ground cinnamon

1 tablespoon honey or maple syrup

1 tablespoon chia seeds

1 cup ice cubes

Nutritional Information (Per Serving): Calories: 220| Total Fat: 10g| Saturated Fat: 8g| Cholesterol: 0mg| Protein: 3g| Sodium: 20mg| Carbohydrates: 30g| Dietary Fiber: 4g| Sugar: 18g

Hints and Tactics

For visual appeal, sprinkle some more turmeric on top as a garnish. Try adding a tiny bit of black pepper to see if that improves the absorption of turmeric.

Direction

1. In the Ninja Creami blending pitcher, combine banana, coconut milk, turmeric powder, ground cinnamon, honey (or maple syrup), and chia seeds.

2. Secure the blending pitcher onto the Ninja Creami base and blend on medium speed until the mixture is smooth.

3. Add ice cubes and blend again until the smoothie reaches a refreshing and chilled consistency.

4. Pour into glasses and savor the soothing goodness of the Golden Milk Smoothie.

Broccoli Bliss Smoothie

Embrace the goodness of greens with the Broccoli Bliss smoothie, a nutrient-packed blend that combines the health benefits of broccoli with the richness of almond butter. This protein-rich concoction is both satisfying and wholesome.

Prep Time: 7 minutes| Serves: 2 servings

Ingredients

1 cup steamed broccoli florets, cooled

1 banana

1/4 cup almond butter

1 cup unsweetened almond milk

1 tablespoon chia seeds

1 tablespoon maple syrup

1 cup ice cubes

Nutritional Information (Per Serving): Calories: 250| Fat: 15g| Saturated Fat: 1g| Cholesterol: 0mg| Protein: 9g| Sodium: 80mg| Carbohydrates: 26g| Dietary Fiber: 6g| Sugar: 12g

Hints and Tactics

Change the sweetness by modifying the quantity of maple syrup used. Before blending, make sure the broccoli florets are completely cooled.

Direction

1. In the Ninja Creami blending pitcher, combine steamed broccoli florets, banana, almond butter, almond milk, chia seeds, and maple syrup.
2. Secure the blending pitcher onto the Ninja Creami base and blend on medium speed until the mixture is smooth.
3. Add ice cubes and blend again until the smoothie reaches a creamy and chilled consistency.
4. Pour into glasses and enjoy the nutrient-rich goodness of the Broccoli Bliss.

Embark on a journey of exotic flavors with the Dragon Fruit Delight Smoothie. Featuring the vibrant and nutrient-packed dragon fruit, this refreshing smoothie combines tropical fruits and a touch of sweetness for a delightful and visually stunning beverage.

Prep Time: 5 minutes| Serves:| 2 servings

Ingredient

1 cup frozen dragon fruit chunks

1 cup frozen pineapple chunks

1 ripe banana

1/2 cup coconut milk

1 tablespoon honey or agave syrup

1 cup water

Ice cubes (optional)

Nutritional Information (Per Serving): Calories: 150| Fat: 2g| Saturated Fat: 1g| Cholesterol: 0mg| Protein: 2g| Sodium: 20mg| Carbohydrates: 35g| Dietary Fiber: 5g| Sugar: 20g

Hints and Tactics

Try out various tropical fruits, like passion fruit or mango. For an added touch, place a slice of dragon fruit as a garnish on the rim

Direction

1. In the Ninja Creami blending pitcher, combine frozen dragon fruit chunks, frozen pineapple chunks, ripe banana, coconut milk, honey (or agave syrup), and water.

2. Blend on high speed until the smoothie reaches a vibrant and smooth consistency.

3. If desired, add ice cubes and blend again for a colder texture.

4. Pour into glasses and relish the Dragon Fruit Delight Smoothie.

Transport yourself to a tropical paradise with the Guava Sunrise Smoothie. This vibrant and refreshing blend combines the exotic sweetness of guava with citrusy brightness, creating a delightful sunrise in every sip

Prep Time: 5 minutes| Serves: 2 servings

Ingredients

2 cups ripe guava, peeled and diced

1 cup orange juice

1 ripe banana

1/2 cup Greek yogurt

1 tablespoon honey or agave syrup

1 cup ice cube

Nutritional Information (Per Serving): Calories: 180| Total Fat: 1g| Saturated Fat: 0.5g| Cholesterol: 5mg| Protein: 3g| Sodium: 15mg| Carbohydrates: 40g| Dietary Fiber: 5g|Sugar: 25g

Hints and Tactics

Choose ripe guavas for optimal sweetness and flavor. Change the amount of honey or agave syrup to adjust the taste.

Direction

1. In the Ninja Creami blending pitcher, combine ripe guava, orange juice, ripe banana, Greek yogurt, and honey (or agave syrup).
2. Add ice cubes to the blender for a frostier texture.
3. Blend on high speed until the smoothie reaches a smooth and creamy consistency.
4. Pour into glasses and enjoy the tropical delight of the Guava Sunrise Smoothie.

Refresh and rejuvenate with the Cucumber Cooler, a hydrating and protein-rich smoothie that combines the crispness of cucumber with the creaminess of Greek yogurt. This cool and invigorating drink is a perfect way to stay hydrated and nourished.

Prep Time: 5 minutes| Serves: 2 servings

Ingredients

1 large cucumber, peeled and sliced

1 cup Greek yogurt

1/2 cup coconut water

1 tablespoon fresh mint leaves

1 tablespoon honey

1 cup ice cubes

Nutritional Information (Per Serving): Calories: 150| Fat: 5g| Saturated Fat: 3g| Cholesterol: 15mg| Protein: 8g| Sodium: 40mg| Carbohydrates: 20g| Dietary Fiber: 2g| Sugar: 15g

Hints and Tactics

Before blending, freeze cucumber slices for added coldness. Add a sprig of mint as a garnish for an eye-catching display.

Direction

1. In the Ninja Creami blending pitcher, combine sliced cucumber, Greek yogurt, coconut water, fresh mint leaves, and honey.

2. Secure the blending pitcher onto the Ninja Creami base and blend on medium speed until the mixture is smooth.

3. Add ice cubes and blend again until the smoothie reaches a cool and frothy consistency.

4. Pour into glasses and relish the revitalizing taste of the Cucumber Cooler.

Pineapple Protein Tropical Swirl Ice Cream

Transport yourself to a tropical paradise with the Pineapple Protein Tropical Swirl Ice Cream. Bursting with the exotic flavors of pineapple and coconut, this protein-packed treat is a refreshing escape that brings a taste of the tropics to your dessert bowl.

Prep Time: 15 minutes| Freezing Time: Overnight| Serves: 4

Ingredients

2 cups frozen pineapple chunks

1 cup unsweetened coconut milk

2 scoops vanilla protein powder

1/4 cup shredded coconut

1/3 cup honey or agave syrup

1 teaspoon lime zest

1 tablespoon lime juice

Nutritional Information (Per Serving): Calories: 180| Total Fat: 7g| Saturated Fat: 5g| Cholesterol: 10mg| Protein: 20g| Sodium: 30mg| Carbohydrates: 20g Dietary Fiber: 2g| Sugar: 15g

Hints and Tactics

To boost the tropical essence, incorporate a dash of coconut or pineapple extract. To achieve a smoother consistency, mix in a frozen banana along with the pineapple chunks.

Direction

1. In the Ninja Creami blending pitcher, combine frozen pineapple chunks, coconut milk, vanilla protein powder, shredded coconut, honey (or agave syrup), lime zest, and lime juice.

2. Secure the blending pitcher onto the Ninja Creami base and blend on medium speed until smooth.

3. Transfer the mixture to the Ninja Creami freezing container.

4. Attach the freezing container to the base, select the 'Ice Cream' setting, and let the Ninja Creami freeze the mixture overnight.

5. The next day, scoop the tropical swirl ice cream into bowls or cones.

6. Garnish with additional shredded coconut or fresh pineapple if desired.

Unleash the chocolatey goodness with Chocolate Protein Power Ice Cream. This rich and indulgent frozen treat combines the bold flavor of chocolate with a protein-packed punch, delivering a satisfying and nourishing dessert experience.

Prep Time: 20minutes| Freezing Time: Overnight| Serve 4 Serving

Ingredients

2 cups whole milk

2 scoops chocolate-flavored protein powder

1/3 cup cocoa powder

1/4 cup dark chocolate chips

1/3 cup honey or agave syrup

1 teaspoon vanilla extract

Nutritional Information (Per Serving): Calories: 240| Total Fat: 10g| Saturated Fat: 5g| Cholesterol: 20mg| Protein: 22g| Sodium: 80mg| Carbohydrates: 25g| Dietary Fiber: 3g| Sugar: 18g

Hints and Tactics

Swirl in extra chocolate sauce during the last minute of freezing for added decadence. Top with chopped nuts for a delightful crunch.

Direction

1. In the Ninja Creami blending pitcher, combine whole milk, chocolate-flavored protein powder, cocoa powder, dark chocolate chips, honey (or agave syrup), and vanilla extract.
2. Secure the blending pitcher onto the Ninja Creami base and blend on medium speed until the mixture is smooth.
3. Transfer the chocolate-infused mixture to the Ninja Creami freezing container.
4. Attach the freezing container to the base, select the 'Ice Cream' setting, and let it churn until creamy.
5. Transfer the ice cream to a lidded container and freeze overnight for optimal texture.
6. Let the ice cream soften slightly at room temperature before serving.
7. Scoop, serve, and relish in the Chocolate Protein Power.

Vanilla Almond Protein Swirl Ice Cream

Delight in the harmonious blend of vanilla and almonds with the Vanilla Almond Protein Swirl Ice Cream. This creamy and protein-rich frozen treat offers a subtle sweetness with a satisfying almond crunch, creating a dessert experience worth savoring.

Prep Time: 15 minutes| Freezing Time: Overnight| Serves: 4

Ingredients

2 cups almond milk

2 scoops vanilla protein powder

1/3 cup sliced almonds

1/4 cup honey or agave syrup

1 teaspoon almond extract

1 teaspoon vanilla extract

Nutritional Information (Per Serving):| Calories: 210| Total Fat: 8g| Saturated Fat: 0.5g| Cholesterol: 5mg| Protein: 20g| Sodium: 90mg|Carbohydrates: 25g| Dietary Fiber: 2g| Sugar: 20g

Hints and Tactics

Enhance the nutty flavor by toasting the sliced almonds and add a drizzle of honey or almond butter before serving.

Direction

1. In the Ninja Creami blending pitcher, combine almond milk, vanilla protein powder, sliced almonds, honey (or agave syrup), almond extract, and vanilla extract.

2. Secure the blending pitcher onto the Ninja Creami base and blend on medium speed until the mixture is smooth.

3. Transfer the almond-infused mixture to the Ninja Creami freezing container.

4. Attach the freezing container to the base, select the 'Ice Cream' setting, and let it churn until creamy.

5. Transfer the ice cream to a lidded container and freeze overnight for optimal texture.

6. Let the ice cream soften slightly at room temperature before serving.

7. Scoop, serve, and enjoy the Vanilla Almond Protein Swirl.

Experience a burst of fruity goodness with the Blackberry Protein Burst Ice Cream. Packed with antioxidants and protein, this vibrant treat combines the sweetness of blackberries with the creaminess of protein, creating a delightful dessert that's as nutritious as it is delicious.

Prep Time: 15 minutes| Freezing Time: Overnight| Serves: 4

Ingredients

2 cups frozen blackberries

1 cup unsweetened almond milk

2 scoops vanilla protein powder

1/4 cup Greek yogurt

1/3 cup honey or maple syrup

1 teaspoon lemon zest

1 tablespoon lemon juice

Nutritional Information (Per Serving): Calories: 190| Total Fat: 4.5g| Saturated Fat: 0.5g| Cholesterol: 10mg Protein: 22g| Sodium: 40mg| Carbohydrates: 20g| Dietary Fiber: 5g| Sugar: 15g

Hints and Tactics

For added texture, stir in a handful of crushed nuts or granola before freezing.

Explore various combinations of berries to create a range of fruity protein ice cream choices.

Direction

1. In the Ninja Creami blending pitcher, combine frozen blackberries, almond milk, vanilla protein powder, Greek yogurt, honey (or maple syrup), lemon zest, and lemon juice.

2. Secure the blending pitcher onto the Ninja Creami base and blend on medium speed until the mixture is smooth.

3. Transfer the mixture to the Ninja Creami freezing container.

4. Attach the freezing container to the base, select the 'Ice Cream' setting, and let the Ninja Creami freeze the mixture overnight.

5. The next day, scoop the protein burst ice cream into bowls or cones.

6. Consider topping with fresh blackberries or a drizzle of honey for extra sweetness.

Cinnamon Protein Chai Ice Cream

Indulge in the comforting blend of aromatic chai spices with a protein-packed twist in this Cinnamon Protein Chai Ice Cream. This delightful frozen treat is not only a creamy dessert but also a source of nourishing protein.

Prep Time: 15 minutes| Freezing Time: Overnight| Serves: 4

Ingredients

2 cups unsweetened almond milk

2 scoops vanilla protein powder

1 teaspoon ground cinnamon

1/2 teaspoon ground cardamom

1/4 teaspoon ground ginger

1/4 teaspoon ground cloves

1/4 teaspoon ground nutmeg

1/3 cup honey or maple syrup

1 teaspoon vanilla extract

Nutritional Information (Per Serving): Calories: 180| Total Fat: 4g| Saturated Fat: 0.5g| Cholesterol: 10mg| Protein: 20g| Sodium: 120mg| Carbohydrates: 15g| Dietary Fiber: 1g| Sugar: 11g

Hints and Tactics

Explore with different protein powder flavors to add a unique touch. Before serving, sprinkle extra cinnamon on top for an additional burst of flavor.

Direction

1. In the Ninja Creami blending pitcher, combine almond milk, vanilla protein powder, cinnamon, cardamom, ginger, cloves, nutmeg, honey (or maple syrup), and vanilla extract.

2. Secure the blending pitcher onto the Ninja Creami base and blend on medium speed until smooth.

3. Once blended, transfer the mixture to the Ninja Creami freezing container.

4. Attach the freezing container to the base, select the 'Ice Cream' setting, and let it churn until creamy.

5. Transfer the ice cream to a lidded container and freeze overnight for optimal texture.

6. Let the ice cream soften a little at room temperature before serving.

7. Scoop, serve, and savor the protein-rich goodness with a hint of chai spice.

Embark on a dreamy journey of rich chocolate and velvety peanut butter with this Protein-Packed Peanut Butter Cup Dream. A frozen delight that's not only indulgent but also a great source of high-quality protein.

Prep Time: 20 minutes| Freezing Time: Overnight| Serves: 4 people

Ingredients

2 cups unsweetened almond milk

2 scoops chocolate protein powder

1/3 cup natural peanut butter

1/4 cup cocoa powder

1/4 cup honey or agave syrup

1 teaspoon vanilla extract

1/4 cup dark chocolate chips (optional, for garnish)

Nutritional Information (Per Serving): Calories: 230| Total Fat: 11g| Saturated Fat: 2g| Cholesterol: 5mg| Protein: 23g| Sodium: 150mg| Carbohydrates: 17g| Dietary Fiber: 3g| Sugar: 10g

Hints and Tactics

Swirl in extra peanut butter or chocolate sauce for added indulgence. Use different nut butters for varied flavor profiles.

Direction

1. In the Ninja Creami blending pitcher, combine almond milk, chocolate protein powder, peanut butter, cocoa powder, honey (or agave syrup), and vanilla extract.

2. Secure the blending pitcher onto the Ninja Creami base and blend on medium speed until well combined.

3. Once blended, transfer the mixture to the Ninja Creami freezing container.

4. Attach the freezing container to the base, select the 'Ice Cream' setting, and let it churn until creamy.

5. During the last minute of freezing, add dark chocolate chips for a delightful crunch.

6. Transfer the ice cream to a lidded container and freeze overnight for optimal texture.

7. Let the ice cream soften a little at room temperature before serving.

8. Scoop, serve, and relish the decadence of this protein-packed Peanut Butter Cup Dream.

Paradise Ice Cream with Peach Protein

Transport your taste buds to a Peach Protein Paradise with this luscious and protein-packed ice cream. The sweet aroma of ripe peaches combined with the richness of protein creates a frozen delight that's both refreshing and nourishing.

Prep Time: 15 minutes| Freezing Time: Overnight| Serves: 4

Ingredients

2 cups fresh or frozen peaches, peeled and sliced

2 scoops vanilla protein powder

1/3 cup honey or agave syrup

1 cup unsweetened coconut milk

1 teaspoon vanilla extract

A pinch of salt

Nutritional Information (Per Serving): Calories: 190 Total Fat: 4g Saturated Fat: 3g Cholesterol: 5mg Protein: 20g Sodium: 60mg Carbohydrates: 25g Dietary Fiber: 2g Sugar: 21g

Hints and Tactics

For an extra fruity kick, add a handful of fresh peach chunks during the last minute of freezing. Garnish with a mint sprig or a sprinkle of shredded coconut before serving.

Direction

1. In the Ninja Creami blending pitcher, combine peaches, vanilla protein powder, honey (or agave syrup), coconut milk, vanilla extract, and a pinch of salt.
2. Secure the blending pitcher onto the Ninja Creami base and blend on medium speed until the mixture is smooth.
3. Transfer the peach mixture to the Ninja Creami freezing container.
4. Attach the freezing container to the base, select the 'Ice Cream' setting, and let it churn until creamy.
5. Transfer the ice cream to a lidded container and freeze overnight for optimal texture.
6. Let the ice cream soften a little at room temperature before serving.
7. Scoop, serve, and savor the tropical goodness of Peach Protein Paradise.

Elevate your frozen treat experience with the zesty goodness of Lemon Protein Zest Ice Cream. The bright and citrusy flavor, combined with a protein punch, creates a delightful and refreshing dessert.

Prep Time: 15 minutes| Freezing Time: Overnight| Serves: 4

Ingredients

1 cup plain Greek yogurt

2 scoops lemon-flavored protein powder

1/3 cup honey or maple syrup

Zest of 2 lemons

Juice of 1 lemon

1 teaspoon vanilla extract

Nutritional Information (Per Serving): Calories: 180| Total Fat: 2g| Saturated Fat: 1g| Cholesterol: 10mg| Protein: 22g| Sodium: 60mg| Carbohydrates: 20g| Dietary Fiber: 1g| Sugar: 18g

Hints and Tactics

To enhance the lemon flavor, consider adding additional lemon zest or a hint of lemon extract. Try experimenting with a blend of vanilla and lemon protein powder for a distinctive twist.

Direction

1. In the Ninja Creami blending pitcher, combine Greek yogurt, lemon-flavored protein powder, honey (or maple syrup), lemon zest, lemon juice, and vanilla extract.
2. Secure the blending pitcher onto the Ninja Creami base and blend on medium speed until the mixture is smooth.
3. Transfer the lemony mixture to the Ninja Creami freezing container.
4. Attach the freezing container to the base, select the 'Ice Cream' setting, and let it churn until creamy.
5. Transfer the ice cream to a lidded container and freeze overnight for optimal texture.
6. Let the ice cream soften a little at room temperature before serving.
7. Scoop, serve, and relish the citrusy delight of Lemon Protein Zest.

Indulge in the rich and creamy goodness of Banana Nut Protein Delight Ice Cream. This frozen treat combines the natural sweetness of ripe bananas with the crunch of nuts and the protein punch you need for a delightful and satisfying dessert.

Prep Time: 15 minutes| Freezing Time: Overnight| Serves: 4

Ingredients

3 ripe bananas, peeled and sliced

2 scoops banana-flavored protein powder

1/3 cup chopped walnuts or almonds

1 cup unsweetened almond milk

1/4 cup honey or agave syrup

1 teaspoon vanilla extract

Nutritional Information (Per Serving): Calories: 220| Total Fat: 8g| Saturated Fat: 1g| Cholesterol: 5mg| Protein: 21g| Sodium: 90mg| Carbohydrates: 28g| Dietary Fiber: 3g| Sugar: 17g

Hints and Tactics

If bananas are very ripe, reduce the amount of added sweetener for a naturally sweet treat. Add a touch of nut butter on top before serving to enhance the flavor.

Direction

1. In the Ninja Creami blending pitcher, combine sliced bananas, banana-flavored protein powder, chopped nuts, almond milk, honey (or agave syrup), and vanilla extract.

2. Secure the blending pitcher onto the Ninja Creami base and blend on medium speed until the mixture is smooth.

3. Transfer the banana mixture to the Ninja Creami freezing container.

4. Attach the freezing container to the base, select the 'Ice Cream' setting, and let it churn until creamy.

5. Sprinkle additional chopped nuts during the last minute of freezing for a delightful crunch.

6. Transfer the ice cream to a lidded container and freeze overnight for optimal texture.

7. Let the ice cream soften a little at room temperature before serving.

8. Scoop, serve, and enjoy the Banana Nut Protein Delight.

Immerse yourself in the luscious blend of Cherry Chocolate Protein Fusion Ice Cream. This decadent treat combines the sweetness of cherries with the richness of chocolate, all while providing a protein-packed experience that satisfies your cravings.

Prep Time: 20 minutes| Freezing Time: Overnight| Serves: 4

Ingredients

2 cups frozen cherries, pitted

2 scoops chocolate protein powder

1/3 cup dark chocolate chips

1 cup unsweetened coconut milk

1/4 cup honey or agave syrup

1 teaspoon vanilla extract

Nutritional Information (Per Serving): Calories: 250| Total Fat: 12g| Saturated Fat: 7g| Cholesterol: 5mg| Protein: 20g| Sodium: 60mg| Carbohydrates: 30g| Dietary Fiber: 3g| Sugar: 20g

Hints and Tactics

Get use to different varieties of cherries for flavor variation. Pour chocolate sauce over the top for a decadent finishing touch.

Direction

1. In the Ninja Creami blending pitcher, combine frozen cherries, chocolate protein powder, dark chocolate chips, coconut milk, honey (or agave syrup), and vanilla extract.
2. Secure the blending pitcher onto the Ninja Creami base and blend on medium speed until the mixture is smooth.
3. Transfer the cherry-chocolate mixture to the Ninja Creami freezing container.
4. Attach the freezing container to the base, select the 'Ice Cream' setting, and let it churn until creamy.
5. During the last minute of freezing, add additional chocolate chips for an extra chocolaty experience.
6. Transfer the ice cream to a lidded container and freeze overnight for optimal texture.
7. Let the ice cream soften a little at room temperature before serving.
8. Scoop, serve, and relish the Cherry Chocolate Protein Fusion.

Take the Coconut Protein Swirl Ice Cream and take a tropical trip. This creamy treat adds a protein-rich twist to the rich flavor of coconut. Savor this tropical treat's silky texture and delicate sweetness.

Prep Time: 15 minutes| Freezing Time: Overnight| Serves: 4

Ingredients

1 can (13.5 oz) coconut milk (full-fat)

2 scoops vanilla protein powder

1/3 cup shredded coconut (sweetened or unsweetened)

1/4 cup honey or agave syrup

1 teaspoon coconut extract

A pinch of salt

Nutritional Information (Per Serving): Calories: 230| Total Fat: 16g| Saturated Fat: 14g| Cholesterol: 5mg| Protein: 18g| Sodium: 50mg| Carbohydrates: 16g| Dietary Fiber: 1g| Sugar: 13g

Hints and Tactics

Toasted coconut can be used for added texture and flavor. For an extra coconut kick, add a drizzle of coconut cream or coconut syrup before serving.

Direction

1. In the Ninja Creami blending pitcher, combine coconut milk, vanilla protein powder, shredded coconut, honey (or agave syrup), coconut extract, and a pinch of salt.

2. Secure the blending pitcher onto the Ninja Creami base and blend on medium speed until the mixture is smooth.

3. Transfer the coconut mixture to the Ninja Creami freezing container.

4. Attach the freezing container to the base, select the 'Ice Cream' setting, and let it churn until creamy.

5. Transfer the ice cream to a lidded container and freeze overnight for optimal texture.

6. Let the ice cream soften a little at room temperature before serving.

7. Scoop, serve, and enjoy the tropical bliss of Coconut Protein Swirl.

Satisfy your tropical cravings with the Mango Protein Tropical Temptation Ice Cream. Bursting with the sweetness of ripe mangoes and a protein-packed punch, this frozen delight brings the taste of the tropics to your dessert bowl.

Prep Time: 15 minutes| Freezing Time: Overnight| Serves: 4

Ingredients

2 cups ripe mango, peeled and diced

2 scoops mango-flavored protein powder

1/3 cup plain Greek yogurt

1/4 cup honey or agave syrup

1 cup unsweetened almond milk

1 teaspoon lime zest

1 tablespoon lime juice

Nutritional Information (Per Serving): Calories: 210| Total Fat: 4g| Saturated Fat: 0.5g| Cholesterol: 5mg| Protein: 22g| Sodium: 70mg| Carbohydrates: 25g| Dietary Fiber: 2g| Sugar: 20g

Hints and Tactics

Include fresh mango chunks in the final minute of freezing for an extra layer of texture. Explore a hint of chili powder to give your frozen treat a spicy mango twist.

Direction

1. In the Ninja Creami blending pitcher, combine diced mango, mango-flavored protein powder, Greek yogurt, honey (or agave syrup), almond milk, lime zest, and lime juice.

2. Secure the blending pitcher onto the Ninja Creami base and blend on medium speed until the mixture is smooth.

3. Transfer the mango mixture to the Ninja Creami freezing container.

4. Attach the freezing container to the base, select the 'Ice Cream' setting, and let it churn until creamy.

5. Transfer the ice cream to a lidded container and freeze overnight for optimal texture.

6. Before serving, allow the ice cream to soften slightly at room temperature.

7. Scoop, serve, and indulge in the tropical temptation of Mango Protein Ice Cream.

The Caramel Fudge Protein Indulgence Ice Cream will satisfy both your cravings for protein and your sweet palate. This delicious frozen delicacy combines rich fudge with creamy caramel swirls for a delightfully sweet and protein-rich taste.

Prep Time: 20 minutes| Freezing Time: Overnight| Serves: 4

Ingredients

1 can (13.5 oz) full-fat coconut milk

2 scoops chocolate protein powder

1/3 cup caramel sauce (plus extra for swirling)

1/4 cup dark chocolate chips

1/4 cup chopped nuts (walnuts or pecans)

1 teaspoon vanilla extract

Nutritional Information (Per Serving): Calories: 280| Total Fat: 20g| Saturated Fat: 15g| Cholesterol: 5mg| Protein: 15g| Sodium: 50mg| Carbohydrates: 20g| Dietary Fiber: 2g| Sugar: 15g

Hints and Tactics

Toasted nuts add a delightful crunch; consider adding them as a topping. Get use to different types of caramel sauce for varied flavor profiles.

Direction

1. In the Ninja Creami blending pitcher, combine coconut milk, chocolate protein powder, caramel sauce, dark chocolate chips, chopped nuts, and vanilla extract.

2. Secure the blending pitcher onto the Ninja Creami base and blend on medium speed until the mixture is smooth.

3. Transfer the indulgent mixture to the Ninja Creami freezing container.

4. Attach the freezing container to the base, select the 'Ice Cream' setting, and let it churn until creamy.

5. Drizzle additional caramel sauce during the last minute of freezing for a caramel swirl effect.

6. Transfer the ice cream to a lidded container and freeze overnight for optimal texture.

7. Before serving, allow the ice cream to soften slightly at room temperature.

8. Scoop, serve, and relish in the Caramel Fudge Protein Indulgence.

With this luscious, protein-packed ice cream, take a trip to Pistachio Protein Paradise. Pistachios have a unique flavor and velvety texture that come together to provide a delicious frozen treat that is both healthy and decadent.

Prep Time: 15 minutes| Freezing Time: Overnight| Serves: 4

Ingredients

1 cup shelled pistachios

2 scoops vanilla protein powder

1/3 cup honey or agave syrup

1 can (13.5 oz) full-fat coconut milk

1 teaspoon almond extract

A pinch of salt

Nutritional Information (Per Serving): Calories: 260| Total Fat: 18g| Saturated Fat: 10g| Cholesterol: 5mg| Protein: 13g| Sodium: 40mg| Carbohydrates: 20g| Dietary Fiber: 2g| Sugar: 15g

Hints and Tactics

I preferred a touch of rose water for a unique flavor twist. Add a drizzle of honey or pistachio sauce to boost the sweetness.

Direction

1. In the Ninja Creami blending pitcher, combine shelled pistachios, vanilla protein powder, honey (or agave syrup), coconut milk, almond extract, and a pinch of salt.

2. Secure the blending pitcher onto the Ninja Creami base and blend on medium speed until the mixture is smooth.

3. Transfer the pistachio mixture to the Ninja Creami freezing container.

4. Attach the freezing container to the base, select the 'Ice Cream' setting, and let it churn until creamy.

5. Transfer the ice cream to a lidded container and freeze overnight for optimal texture.

6. Before serving, allow the ice cream to soften slightly at room temperature.

7. Scoop, serve, and savor the Pistachio Protein Paradise.

Experience the blissful union of cookies and cream with this protein-packed delight. Cookies and Cream Protein Bliss Ice Cream offers a velvety texture, rich chocolate goodness, and the added bonus of a protein punch for a truly indulgent frozen treat.

Prep Time: 20 minutes| Freezing Time: Overnight| Serves: 4

Ingredients

2 cups unsweetened almond milk

2 scoops cookies and cream-flavored protein powder

1/2 cup crushed chocolate sandwich cookies

1/4 cup dark chocolate chips

1/3 cup honey or agave syrup

1 teaspoon vanilla extract

Nutritional Information (Per Serving): Calories: 240| Total Fat: 10g| Saturated Fat: 4g| Cholesterol: 5mg| Protein: 22g| Sodium: 130mg| Carbohydrates: 26g| Dietary Fiber: 2g| Sugar: 18g

Hints and Tactics

For a double cookie crunch, mix in extra crushed cookies during the last minute of freezing. Garnish with a drizzle of chocolate sauce or cookie crumbs for a decorative touch.

Directions

1. In the Ninja Creami blending pitcher, combine almond milk, cookies and cream-flavored protein powder, crushed chocolate sandwich cookies, dark chocolate chips, honey (or agave syrup), and vanilla extract.

2. Secure the blending pitcher onto the Ninja Creami base and blend on medium speed until the mixture is smooth.

3. Transfer the cookie-infused mixture to the Ninja Creami freezing container.

4. Attach the freezing container to the base, select the 'Ice Cream' setting, and let it churn until creamy.

5. Transfer the ice cream to a lidded container and fold in additional crushed cookies for texture.

6. Freeze the ice cream overnight for optimal texture.

7. Let the ice cream soften a little at room temperature before serving.

8. Scoop, serve, and savor the Cookies and Cream Protein Bliss.

Delight your taste buds with the sweet-tart goodness of Raspberry Ripple Protein Delight Ice Cream. This protein-packed frozen treat combines the vibrant flavors of ripe raspberries with a velvety base for a refreshing and indulgent dessert experience.

Prep Time: 15 minutes| Freezing Time: Overnight| Serves: 4

Ingredients

2 cups fresh or frozen raspberries

2 scoops vanilla protein powder

1/3 cup honey or agave syrup

1 cup plain Greek yogurt

1 teaspoon vanilla extract

Nutritional Information (Per Serving): Calories: 190| Total Fat: 2g| Saturated Fat: 0.5g| Cholesterol: 5mg| Protein: 20g| Sodium: 40mg| Carbohydrates: 25g| Dietary Fiber: 5g| Sugar: 18g

Hints and Tactics

Add a handful of fresh raspberries during the last minute of freezing for a burst of texture. For a final touch, add a sprinkling of powdered sugar or a mint leaf.

Direction

1. In the Ninja Creami blending pitcher, combine raspberries, vanilla protein powder, honey (or agave syrup), Greek yogurt, and vanilla extract.
2. Secure the blending pitcher onto the Ninja Creami base and blend on medium speed until the mixture is smooth.
3. Transfer the raspberry-infused mixture to the Ninja Creami freezing container.
4. Attach the freezing container to the base, select the 'Ice Cream' setting, and let it churn until creamy.
5. Drizzle additional honey or agave syrup during the last minute of freezing for a sweet ripple effect.
6. Transfer the ice cream to a lidded container and freeze overnight for optimal texture.
7. Let the ice cream soften a little at room temperature before serving.
8. Scoop, serve, and enjoy the Raspberry Ripple Protein Delight.

Strawberry Protein Blast Ice Cream

Experience a burst of fruity delight with the Strawberry Protein Blast Ice Cream. This frozen treat combines the sweetness of ripe strawberries with a protein-packed punch, creating a refreshing and satisfying dessert.

Prep Time: 15 minutes| Freezing Time: Overnight| Serves: 4

Ingredients

2 cups fresh or frozen strawberries, hulled

2 scoops strawberry-flavored protein powder

1/3 cup honey or agave syrup

1 cup unsweetened coconut milk

1 teaspoon vanilla extract

Nutritional Information (Per Serving): Calories: 180| Total Fat: 4g| Saturated Fat: 3g| Cholesterol: 5mg| Protein: 20g| Sodium: 60mg| Carbohydrates: 15g| Dietary Fiber: 2g| Sugar: 10g

Hints and Tactics

Add a handful of diced strawberries during the last minute of freezing for extra texture. Modify the level of sweetness by adjusting the quantity of honey or agave syrup used.

Direction

1. In the Ninja Creami blending pitcher, combine strawberries, strawberry-flavored protein powder, honey (or agave syrup), coconut milk, and vanilla extract.
2. Secure the blending pitcher onto the Ninja Creami base and blend on medium speed until the mixture is smooth.
3. Transfer the strawberry-infused mixture to the Ninja Creami freezing container.
4. Attach the freezing container to the base, select the 'Ice Cream' setting, and let it churn until creamy.
5. Transfer the ice cream to a lidded container and freeze overnight for optimal texture.
6. Let the ice cream soften a little at room temperature before serving.
7. Scoop, serve, and enjoy the Strawberry Protein Blast.

Coffee Protein Punch Ice Cream

Elevate your dessert experience with the Coffee Protein Punch Ice Cream. This rich and creamy treat combines the bold flavor of coffee with a protein-packed twist, providing a delightful pick-me-up in frozen form.

Prep Time: 15 minutes| Freezing Time: Overnight| Serves: 4

Ingredients

1 cup strong brewed coffee, cooled

2 scoops coffee-flavored protein powder

1/3 cup honey or agave syrup

1 cup whole milk

1 teaspoon vanilla extract

Nutritional Information (Per Serving): Calories: 220 Total Fat: 8g Saturated Fat: 5g Cholesterol: 15mg Protein: 18g Sodium: 60mg Carbohydrates: 20g Dietary Fiber: 0g Sugar: 18g

Hints and Tactics

For an extra coffee kick, add a shot of espresso or coffee extract. Finish it off by topping it with a dusting of cocoa powder or chocolate shavings for an added touch.

Direction

1. In the Ninja Creami blending pitcher, combine cooled brewed coffee, coffee-flavored protein powder, honey (or agave syrup), whole milk, and vanilla extract.
2. Secure the blending pitcher onto the Ninja Creami base and blend on medium speed until the mixture is smooth.
3. Transfer the coffee-infused mixture to the Ninja Creami freezing container.
4. Attach the freezing container to the base, select the 'Ice Cream' setting, and let it churn until creamy.
5. Transfer the ice cream to a lidded container and freeze overnight for optimal texture.
6. Let the ice cream soften a little at room temperature before serving.
7. Scoop, serve, and enjoy the Coffee Protein Punch.

Spiced Latte Protein Shake

Start your day with the warm and inviting flavors of a Spiced Latte Protein Shake. This protein-packed beverage combines the richness of coffee with a blend of warm spices, creating a satisfying and energizing treat.

Prep Time: 5 minutes| Serves: 2 servings

Ingredients

1 cup strong brewed coffee, cooled

1 cup milk of your choice (dairy or plant-based)

2 scoops vanilla or spiced latte-flavored protein powder

1 tablespoon maple syrup or honey

1/2 teaspoon ground cinnamon

1/4 teaspoon ground nutmegs

Ice cubes (optional)

Nutritional Information (Per Serving): Calories: 180| Total Fat: 5g| Saturated Fat: 3g| Cholesterol: 20mg| Protein: 20g| Sodium: 90mg| Carbohydrates: 15g| Dietary Fiber: 1g| Sugar: 10g

Hints & Tactics

Taste and adjust the amount of sweetness and spice to suit your needs. Top with a sprinkle of cinnamon or a dollop of whipped cream for an extra treat.

Direction

1. In the Ninja Creami blending pitcher, combine cooled brewed coffee, milk, protein powder, maple syrup (or honey), ground cinnamon, and ground nutmeg.

2. Blend on high speed until all ingredients are well combined and the shake is smooth.

3. To achieve a colder consistency, feel free to add ice cubes and blend once more.

4. Pour into glasses, and enjoy the invigorating flavors of your Spiced Latte Protein Shake.

Indulge in the fruity sweetness of a Vanilla Berry Protein Shake. This refreshing beverage combines the classic taste of vanilla with the vibrant flavors of mixed berries, offering a delicious and protein-packed way to kick-start your day.

Prep Time: 5 minutes| Serves: 2 servings

Ingredients

1 cup mixed berries (strawberries, blueberries, raspberries)

1 cup milk of your choice (dairy or plant-based)

2 scoops vanilla-flavored protein powder

1 tablespoon honey or agave syrup

1/2 teaspoon vanilla extract

Ice cubes (optional)

Nutritional Information (Per Serving): Calories: 200| Total Fat: 4g| Saturated Fat: 2g| Cholesterol: 15mg| Protein: 22g| Sodium: 80mg| Carbohydrates: 20g| Dietary Fiber: 4g| Sugar: 15g

Hints & Tactics

Tailor the assortment of berries according to your preferences. Add a touch of elegance by decorating with a handful of intact berries for an aesthetically pleasing display.

Direction

1. In the Ninja Creami blending pitcher, combine mixed berries, milk, protein powder, honey (or agave syrup), and vanilla extract.

2. Blend on high speed until the shake is smooth and the berries are fully incorporated.

3. If desired, add ice cubes and blend again for a colder consistency.

4. Pour into glasses, and savor the delightful flavors of your Vanilla Berry Protein Shake.

Coconut Protein Colada Shake

Transport yourself to a tropical paradise with the Coconut Protein Colada Shake. This refreshing and protein-packed beverage combines the luscious flavor of coconut with a hint of pineapple, creating a delightful shake that's both nourishing and indulgent.

Prep Time: 5 minutes| Serves: 2 servings

Ingredients

2 cups coconut milk

1 scoop vanilla protein powder

1/2 cup frozen pineapple chunks

1/4 cup shredded coconut (unsweetened)

1 tablespoon honey or agave syrup

1/2 teaspoon coconut extract (optional)

Ice cubes (optional)

Nutritional Information (Per Serving): Calories: 220| Total Fat: 12g| Saturated Fat: 10g| Cholesterol: 5mg| Protein: 20g| Sodium: 40mg| Carbohydrates: 15g| Dietary Fiber: 1g| Sugar: 10g

Hints and Tactics

Utilize frozen pineapple for a more frozen texture, and customize the sweetness and coconut flavor to your liking.

Direction

1. In the Ninja Creami blending pitcher, combine coconut milk, vanilla protein powder, frozen pineapple chunks, shredded coconut, honey (or agave syrup), and coconut extract.
2. Blend the ingredients until the mixture is smooth and creamy.
3. If desired, add ice cubes and blend again until the shake reaches your preferred consistency.
4. Pour the Coconut Protein Colada Shake into glasses.
5. Serve immediately and enjoy the tropical goodness.

Indulge in the comforting flavors of an Oatmeal Cookie Latte, a protein-rich twist on a classic favorite. This beverage combines the warmth of oatmeal, the sweetness of cookies, and the kick of a latte for a delightful treat that's both satisfying and nourishing.

Prep Time: 10 minutes| Cooking Time: 5 minutes| Serves: 2 servings

Ingredients

1 cup brewed coffee

1 cup of your preferred milk (vegan or dairy)

2 scoops vanilla protein powder

1/4 cup rolled oats

2 tablespoons maple syrup or honey

1/2 teaspoon ground cinnamon

1/4 teaspoon vanilla extract

Whipped cream and cinnamon for garnish (optional)

Nutritional Information (Per Serving): Calories: 220| Total Fat: 5g| Saturated Fat: 2g| Cholesterol: 20mg| Protein: 22g| Sodium: 80mg| Carbohydrates: 25g| Dietary Fiber: 2g| Sugar: 12g

Hints and Tactics

Adjust the sweetness by incorporating additional or reducing the amount of honey or maple syrup. Enhance the texture further by sprinkling a handful of crushed oatmeal cookies on top.

Direction

1. In the Ninja Creami blending pitcher, combine brewed coffee, oat milk, vanilla protein powder, rolled oats, maple syrup (or sweetener), ground cinnamon, and vanilla extract.

2. Blend the ingredients until the mixture is smooth and well combined.

3. Pour the Oatmeal Cookie Latte into a mug.

4. If desired, top with whipped cream and a sprinkle of cinnamon for extra indulgence.

5. Serve immediately and savor the comforting blend of oatmeal cookie goodness with a caffeine boost.

Savor the delightful flavors of a Blueberry Muffin Blast, a protein-packed smoothie inspired by the classic baked treat. This refreshing beverage combines the sweetness of blueberries with the comforting essence of a muffin, creating a nourishing and satisfying drink.

Prep Time: 5 minutes| Serves: 2 servings

Ingredients

1 cup fresh or frozen blueberries

1 ripe banana

1 cup vanilla Greek yogurt

2 scoops vanilla protein powder

1/2 cup rolled oats

1 tablespoon honey or agave syrup

1/2 teaspoon ground cinnamon

Ice cubes (optional)

Nutritional Information (Per Serving): Calories: 220| Total Fat: 3g| Saturated Fat: 1g| Cholesterol: 15mg| Protein: 20g| Sodium: 50mg| Carbohydrates: 35g| Dietary Fiber: 5g| Sugar: 18g

Hints & Tactics

Modify the amount of honey or agave syrup to suit your preferred level of sweetness. Before serving, sprinkle a few more rolled oats over top for some texture

Direction

1. In the Ninja Creami blending pitcher, combine blueberries, ripe banana, vanilla Greek yogurt, vanilla protein powder, rolled oats, honey (or agave syrup), and ground cinnamon.

2. Secure the blending pitcher onto the Ninja Creami base and blend on medium speed until the mixture is smooth and creamy.

3. If desired, add ice cubes and blend again for a colder consistency.

4. Pour into glasses and relish the delightful Blueberry Muffin Blast.

Indulge in the rich and creamy goodness of a Chocolate Avocado Protein Shake. This delectable and protein-packed beverage combines the velvety texture of ripe avocados with the bold flavor of chocolate, creating a nourishing and satisfying shake.

Prep Time: 5 minutes| Serves: 2 servings

Ingredients

1 ripe avocado, peeled and pitted

2 cups milk of your choice (dairy or plant-based)

2 scoops chocolate-flavored protein powder

2 tablespoons cocoa powder

2 tablespoons honey or agave syrup

1/2 teaspoon vanilla extract

Ice cubes (optional)

Nutritional Information (Per Serving): Calories: 300| Total Fat: 15g| Saturated Fat: 3g| Cholesterol: 10mg| Protein: 22g| Sodium: 100mg| Carbohydrates: 30g| Dietary Fiber: 8g| Sugar: 18g

Hints & Tactics

For an extra nutritional boost, add a handful of spinach or kale. For a final touch, sprinkle some cocoa powder or grated chocolate on top.

Direction

1. In the Ninja Creami blending pitcher, combine ripe avocado, almond milk, chocolate protein powder, cocoa powder, almond butter, honey (or maple syrup), and vanilla extract.

2. Blend the ingredients until the shake is smooth and creamy.

3. If desired, add ice cubes and blend again until the shake reaches your preferred consistency.

4. Pour the Chocolate Avocado Protein Shake into glasses.

5. Optionally, garnish with a sprinkle of cocoa powder or a dollop of whipped cream.

6. Serve immediately and savor the chocolaty indulgence.

Peppermint Bark Milkshake

Delight in the festive spirit with a Peppermint Bark Milkshake, a refreshing and indulgent treat that captures the essence of the holiday season. This cool and creamy shake combines the classic flavors of peppermint and chocolate, creating a blissful sip-worthy experience.

Prep Time: 10 minutes| Serves: 2 servings

Ingredients

2 cups vanilla ice cream

1 cup of your preferred milk (vegan or dairy)

1/2 cup crushed peppermint bark or candy canes

2 scoops chocolate protein powder

1/2 teaspoon peppermint extract

Whipped cream and additional crushed peppermint for garnish (optional)

Nutritional Information (Per Serving): Calories: 350| Total Fat: 18g| Saturated Fat: 10g| Cholesterol: 45mg| Protein: 20g| Sodium: 120mg| Carbohydrates: 40g| Dietary Fiber: 2g| Sugar: 30g.

Hints and Tactics

Modify the quantity of peppermint extract to match your desired intensity of peppermint flavor. You can try different types of milk to attain diverse levels of richness.

Direction

1. In the Ninja Creami blending pitcher, combine milk, chocolate protein powder, crushed peppermint candies, chocolate syrup, peppermint extract, and vanilla ice cream.

2. Blend the ingredients until the milkshake reaches a smooth and creamy consistency.

3. Pour the Peppermint Bark Milkshake into glasses.

4. If desired, top with whipped cream and sprinkle additional crushed peppermint on top for garnish.

5. Serve immediately, and savor the festive and protein-rich goodness.

Celebrate the spirit of St. Patrick's Day with a refreshing and festive Shamrock Shake. This green-hued delight combines the flavors of mint and vanilla in a creamy concoction, making it a delightful treat for the season.

Prep Time: 5 minutes| Serves: 2 servings

Ingredients

2 cups almond milk (or milk of choice)

1 scoop vanilla protein powder

1/2 teaspoon peppermint extract

1/4 teaspoon spirulina powder (for color, optional)

1 tablespoon honey or maple syrup

1/2 teaspoon vanilla extract

Ice cubes

Nutritional Information (Per Serving): Calories: 200| Total Fat: 15g| Saturated Fat: 1g| Cholesterol: 0mg| Protein: 15g| Sodium: 100mg|| Carbohydrates: 20g| Dietary Fiber: 0g| Sugar: 15g

Hints & Tactics

For an extra creamy texture, consider adding a frozen banana. If spirulina powder is not available, a few drops of green food coloring can be used for color.

Direction

1. In the Ninja Creami blending pitcher, combine almond milk, vanilla protein powder, peppermint extract, spirulina powder (if using), honey (or maple syrup), and vanilla extract.

2. Blend the ingredients until the mixture is smooth and creamy.

3. After adding the ice cubes, combine the shake once more to get the desired consistency.

4. Pour the Shamrock Shake into glasses.

5. Garnish with a sprig of fresh mint or a dusting of spirulina powder if desired.

6. Serve immediately and enjoy the festive flavors.

Kahlua Mocha Milkshake

Indulge in the rich and adult flavors of a Kahlua Mocha Milkshake, a delightful blend of coffee, chocolate, and a hint of Kahlua liqueur. This boozy and decadent milkshake is perfect for a grown-up treat or a special dessert occasion.

Prep Time: 10 minutes| Serves: 2 servings

Ingredients

1 cup cold brew coffee

1/2 cup milk (dairy or plant-based)

2 scoops chocolate protein powder

2 tablespoons chocolate syrup

1 tablespoon Kahlua (optional)

1 tablespoon unsweetened cocoa powder

1 teaspoon vanilla extract

Ice cubes

Nutritional Information (Per Serving): Calories: 200| Total Fat: 6g| Saturated Fat: 3| Cholesterol: 25mg| Protein: 15g| Sodium: 75mg| Carbohydrates: 25g| Dietary Fiber: 2g| Sugar: 15g

Hints & Tactics

For a non-alcoholic version, omit the Kahlua and increase the vanilla extract. Add a touch of extravagance by topping it with whipped cream and chocolate shavings.

Directions

1. In the Ninja Creami blending pitcher, combine cold brew coffee, milk, chocolate protein powder, chocolate syrup, Kahlua (if using), cocoa powder, and vanilla extract.

2. Blend the ingredients until the mixture is smooth and creamy.

3. Add ice cubes and blend again until the milkshake reaches your desired thickness.

4. Pour the Kahlua Mocha Milkshake into glasses.

5. Drizzle extra chocolate syrup on top for a decorative touch.

6. Serve immediately and savor the delightful combination of rich flavors.

Experience the warm and comforting flavors of fall with the Autumn Glow Milkshake. This seasonal delight combines the richness of spiced pumpkin, the sweetness of caramel, and a hint of cinnamon for a deliciously spiced treat that captures the essence of autumn.

Prep Time: 10 minutes| Serves: 2 servings

Ingredients

2 cups almond milk

1 scoop vanilla protein powder

1/2 cup canned pumpkin puree

1/2 teaspoon pumpkin spice

1 tablespoon maple syrup

1/2 teaspoon vanilla extract

Ice cubes (optional)

Whipped cream and cinnamon for garnish (optional)

Nutritional Information (Per Serving): Calories: 180| Total Fat: 1g| Saturated Fat: 10g| Cholesterol: 50mg| Protein: 15g| Sodium: 180mg| Carbohydrates: 0g| Dietary Fiber: 5g| Sugar: 10g

Direction

1. In the Ninja Creami blending pitcher, combine almond milk, vanilla protein powder, canned pumpkin puree, pumpkin spice, maple syrup, and vanilla extract.

2. Blend the ingredients until the mixture is smooth and creamy.

3. If a colder shake is desired, add ice cubes and blend again until the desired consistency is reached.

4. Pour the Autumn Glow Milkshake into glasses.

5. Optionally, top with a dollop of whipped cream and a sprinkle of cinnamon for an extra autumn touch.

6. Serve immediately and savor the cozy flavors of fall.

Hints and Tactics

To enhance the texture, you might want to incorporate a handful of rolled oats or chia seeds. Feel free to experiment with a hint of nutmeg or cloves to introduce an additional layer of spice.

Indulge in the velvety goodness of a Choco Cream Cheese Milkshake, a decadent blend of rich chocolate, creamy cheese, and a touch of sweetness. This luscious milkshake is a delightful treat for chocolate lovers with a creamy twist.

Prep Time: 10 minutes| Serves: 2 servings

Ingredients

2 cups whole milk

1/2 cup cream cheese, softened

2 tablespoons cocoa powder

1/4 cup chocolate protein powder

2 tablespoons honey or maple syrup

1 teaspoon vanilla extract

Ice cubes (optional)

Nutritional Information (Per Serving): Calories: 280| Total Fat: 14g| Saturated Fat: 8g| Cholesterol: 40mg| Protein: 15g| Sodium: 150mg| Carbohydrates: 30g| Dietary Fiber: 2g| Sugar: 25g

Hints and Tactics

Consider adding a scoop of chocolate-flavored ice cream for extra thickness. Try adding a small pinch of cinnamon for a little warmth.

Direction

1. In the Ninja Creami blending pitcher, combine whole milk, softened cream cheese, cocoa powder, chocolate protein powder, honey (or maple syrup), and vanilla extract.

2. Blend the ingredients until the mixture is smooth and creamy.

3. If a colder shake is desired, add ice cubes and blend again until the desired consistency is reached.

4. Pour the Choco Cream Cheese Milkshake into glasses.

5. Optionally, garnish with a sprinkle of cocoa powder or chocolate shavings.

6. Serve immediately

Enjoy the vibrant and tropical flavors of an Orange Banana and Mango Shake. This refreshing and vitamin-packed beverage combines the citrusy brightness of oranges, the creaminess of bananas, and the exotic sweetness of mango for a delightful and healthy treat.

Prep Time: 7 minutes| Serves: 2 servings

Ingredients

1 cup orange juice

1 cup frozen mango chunks

2 ripe bananas

1 scoop vanilla protein powder

1/2 cup Greek yogurt

1 tablespoon honey or agave syrup

Ice cubes (optional)

Nutritional Information (Per Serving): Calories: 280| Total Fat: 2g| Saturated Fat: 1g| Cholesterol: 5mg| Protein: 20g| Sodium: 40mg| Carbohydrates: 55g| Dietary Fiber: 6g| Sugar: 35g

Hints and Tactics

Change the amount of honey or agave syrup to adjust the sweetness. Try adding a small handful of spinach to add extra nutrients without changing the flavor.

Direction

1. In the Ninja Creami blending pitcher, combine orange juice, frozen mango chunks, ripe bananas, vanilla protein powder, Greek yogurt, and honey (or agave syrup).
2. Blend the ingredients until the mixture is smooth and creamy.
3. If a colder shake is desired, add ice cubes and blend again until the shake reaches the desired temperature and consistency.
4. Pour the Orange Banana and Mango Shake into glasses.
5. Garnish with a slice of orange or a few mango chunks if desired.
6. Serve immediately and enjoy the burst of fruity goodness.

Papaya Passion Protein Sorbet

Experience the vibrant and tropical fusion of Papaya Passion Protein Sorbet, a refreshing and protein-enriched frozen treat that combines the sweetness of papaya with the exotic notes of passion fruit. This sorbet is not only a delightful indulgence but also a nutritious addition to your dessert repertoire.

Prep Time: 15 minutes| Churning Time: 20 minutes| Freezing Time: 24 hours

Ingredients

2 cups ripe papaya, diced

1/2 cup passion fruit puree

1/2 cup Greek yogurt

1/4 cup honey or agave syrup

1 scoop vanilla protein powder
Pinch of salt
Fresh mint leaves for garnish (optional)

Nutritional Information (Per Serving): Calories: 140| Total Fat: 2g| Saturated Fat: 1g| Cholesterol: 10mg| Protein: 6g| Sodium: 30mg| Carbohydrates: 25g| Dietary Fiber: 2g| Sugar: 20g

Hints and Tactics

Enhance the texture by incorporating a handful of diced papaya into the mix before freezing. Explore the addition of a splash of coconut milk for an added layer of creaminess.

Directions

1. In the Ninja Creami blending pitcher, combine diced papaya, passion fruit puree, Greek yogurt, honey (or agave syrup), vanilla protein powder, and a pinch of salt.
2. Secure the blending pitcher onto the Ninja Creami base and blend on medium speed until the mixture is well-combined.
3. Pour the mixture into the Ninja Creami freezing container.
4. Attach the whipping accessory and set the Ninja Creami to "Sorbet" mode.
5. Once the sorbet reaches a creamy consistency, transfer it to an airtight container and freeze for an additional 24 hours to firm up.
6. Serve the Papaya Passion Protein Sorbet in bowls or cones, garnished with fresh mint leaves if desired.

Energize your palate with the vibrant and refreshing Pomegranate Protein Power Sorbet, a delightful frozen treat that combines the tartness of pomegranate with the goodness of protein. This sorbet not only tantalizes your taste buds but also provides a protein-packed boost for a guilt-free indulgence

Prep Time: 15 minutes| Churning Time: 20 minutes| Freezing Time: 24 hours

Ingredients

1 1/2 cups pomegranate juice

1/2 cup plain Greek yogurt

1/4 cup honey or agave syrup

1 scoop vanilla protein powder

1 tablespoon lemon juice

Pinch of salt

Pomegranate arils for garnish (optional)

Nutritional Information (Per Serving): Calories: 120| Total Fat: 1g| Saturated Fat: 0.5g| Cholesterol: 5mg| Protein: 5g| Sodium: 20mg| Carbohydrates: 25g| Dietary Fiber: 1g| Sugar: 20g

Hints and Tactics

Enhance the texture by generously scattering crushed nuts over the dish just before serving. Explore a hint of mint to infuse a revitalizing and unique flavor

Directions

1. In the Ninja Creami blending pitcher, combine pomegranate juice, Greek yogurt, honey (or agave syrup), vanilla protein powder, lemon juice, and a pinch of salt.

2. Secure the blending pitcher onto the Ninja Creami base and blend on medium speed until the mixture is well-combined.

3. Pour the mixture into the Ninja Creami freezing container.

4. Attach the whipping accessory and set the Ninja Creami to "Sorbet" mode.

5. Once the sorbet reaches a creamy consistency, transfer it to an airtight container and freeze for an additional 24 hours to firm up.

6. Serve the Pomegranate Protein Power Sorbet in bowls or cones, garnished with pomegranate arils if desired.

Delight in the sweet and protein-packed goodness of Cantaloupe Protein Melon Sorbet, a refreshing treat that brings together the natural sweetness of cantaloupe with the creaminess of protein-packed ingredients. This sorbet is a guilt-free way to enjoy the essence of summer.

Prep Time: 10 minutes| Churning Time: 15 minutes| Freezing Time: 24 hours| Serves: 4 servings

Ingredients

2 cups ripe cantaloupe, diced

1/2 cup coconut milk

1/4 cup honey or agave syrup

1 scoop vanilla protein powder

Zest of 1 lime

Pinch of salt

Fresh basil leaves for garnish (optional)

Nutritional Information (Per Serving): Calories: 140| Total Fat: 2g| Saturated Fat: 1g| Cholesterol: 10mg| Protein: 7g| Sodium: 30mg| Carbohydrates: 25g| Dietary Fiber: 2g| Sugar: 20g

Hints and Tactics

For added texture, consider mixing in a handful of diced cantaloupe before freezing. Experiment with a touch of fresh mint for a refreshing twist.

Directions

1. In the Ninja Creami blending pitcher, combine diced cantaloupe, coconut milk, honey (or agave syrup), vanilla protein powder, lime zest, and a pinch of salt.

2. Secure the blending pitcher onto the Ninja Creami base and blend on medium speed until the mixture is well-combined.

3. Pour the mixture into the Ninja Creami freezing container.

4. Attach the whipping accessory and set the Ninja Creami to "Sorbet" mode.

5. Once the sorbet reaches a creamy consistency, transfer it to an airtight container and freeze for an additional 24 hours to firm up.

6. Serve the Cantaloupe Protein Melon Sorbet in bowls or cones, garnished with fresh basil leaves if desired.

Revitalize your senses with the Honeydew Mint Protein Refresh Sorbet, a cooling and protein-rich treat that combines the subtle sweetness of honeydew with a burst of refreshing mint. This sorbet is a delightful way to stay cool and nourished.

Prep Time: 10 minutes| Churning Time: 15 minutes| Freezing Time: 4 hours| Serves: 4 servings

Ingredients

2 cups ripe honeydew, diced

1/2 cup plain Greek yogurt

1/4 cup honey or agave syrup

1 scoop vanilla protein powder

1 tablespoon fresh mint leaves, chopped

Zest of 1 lemon

Pinch of salt

Fresh mint leaves for garnish (optional)

Nutritional Information (Per Serving): Calories: 130| Total Fat: 2g| Saturated Fat: 1g| Cholesterol: 10mg| Protein: 6g| Sodium: 30mg| Carbohydrates: 25g| Dietary Fiber: 1g| Sugar: 20g

Hints & Tactics

For an extra burst of freshness, add additional chopped mint before freezing. You can try drizzle of lime juice for added zing.

Directions

1. In the Ninja Creami blending pitcher, combine diced honeydew, Greek yogurt, honey (or agave syrup), vanilla protein powder, chopped fresh mint leaves, lemon zest, and a pinch of salt.

2. Secure the blending pitcher onto the Ninja Creami base and blend on medium speed until the mixture is well-combined.

3. Pour the mixture into the Ninja Creami freezing container.

4. Attach the whipping accessory and set the Ninja Creami to "Sorbet" mode.

5. Once the sorbet reaches a creamy consistency, transfer it to an airtight container and freeze for an additional 4 hours to firm up.

6. Serve the Honeydew Mint Protein Refresh Sorbet in bowls or cones, garnished with fresh mint leaves if desired.

Plum Rosemary Protein Elegance Sorbet

Indulge in sophistication with the Plum Rosemary Protein Elegance Sorbet, a refined and protein-rich treat that marries the deep sweetness of plums with the aromatic touch of rosemary.

Prep Time: 10 minutes| Churning Time: 15 minutes| Freezing Time: 24 hours| Serves: 4 servings

Ingredients

2 cups ripe plums, pitted and diced

1/2 cup water

1/4 cup honey or agave syrup

1 scoop vanilla protein powder

1 tablespoon fresh rosemary leaves, chopped

Zest of 1 lemon

Pinch of salt

Fresh rosemary sprigs for garnish (optional)

Nutritional Information (Per Serving): Calories: 140| Total Fat: 2g| Saturated Fat: 1g| Cholesterol: 10mg| Protein: 7g| Sodium: 30mg| Carbohydrates: 25g| Dietary Fiber: 2g| Sugar: 20g

Hints and Tactics

For an extra layer of sophistication, consider adding a splash of red wine before freezing. Kindly try balsamic reduction for a unique twist.

Directions

1. In the Ninja Creami blending pitcher, combine diced plums, water, honey (or agave syrup), vanilla protein powder, chopped fresh rosemary leaves, lemon zest, and a pinch of salt.

2. Secure the blending pitcher onto the Ninja Creami base and blend on medium speed until the mixture is well-combined.

3. Pour the mixture into the Ninja Creami freezing container.

4. Attach the whipping accessory and set the Ninja Creami to "Sorbet" mode.

5. Once the sorbet reaches a creamy consistency, transfer it to an airtight container and freeze for an additional 24 hours to firm up.

6. Serve the Plum Rosemary Protein Elegance Sorbet in bowls or cones, garnished with fresh rosemary sprigs if desired.

Treat your taste buds to a burst of citrus with the Cranberry Orange Protein Citrus Sorbet, a zesty and protein-rich delight that combines the tartness of cranberries with the vibrant essence of oranges. This sorbet is a refreshing and nutritious way to savor the bright flavors of citrus.

Prep Time: 10 minutes| Churning Time: 15 minutes| Freezing Time: 18 hours| Serves: 2 4 servings

Ingredients	Direction
1 cup fresh cranberries 1 cup orange juice 1/4 cup honey or agave syrup 1 scoop vanilla protein powder Zest of 1 orange Pinch of salt Fresh mint leaves for garnish (optional) Nutritional Information (Per Serving):| Calories: 120| Total Fat: 1g| Saturated Fat: 0.5g| Cholesterol: 5mg| Protein: 6g| Sodium: 20mg| Carbohydrates: 25g|Dietary Fiber: 2g| Sugar: 18g **Hints and Tactics** Change the amount of honey or agave syrup to regulate the sweetness. Before freezing, try adding a handful of diced oranges for some texture.	1. In the Ninja Creami blending pitcher, combine fresh cranberries, orange juice, honey (or agave syrup), vanilla protein powder, orange zest, and a pinch of salt. 2. Secure the blending pitcher onto the Ninja Creami base and blend on medium speed until the mixture is well-combined. 3. Pour the mixture into the Ninja Creami freezing container. 4. Attach the whipping accessory and set the Ninja Creami to "Sorbet" mode. 5. Once the sorbet reaches a creamy consistency, transfer it to an airtight container and freeze for an additional 18 hours to firm up. 6. Serve the Cranberry Orange Protein Citrus Sorbet in bowls or cones, garnished with fresh mint leaves if desired.

Experience the nostalgic warmth of snicker doodle in a guilt-free frozen delight with the Snicker doodle Protein Sorbet. This protein-packed treat combines the classic flavors of cinnamon and vanilla for a refreshing twist on a beloved favorite.

Prep Time: 10 minutes| Churning Time: 15 minutes| Freezing Time: 24 hours| Serves: 4 servings

Ingredients

1 cup almond milk

1/4 cup maple syrup or agave syrup

1 scoop vanilla protein powder

1 teaspoon ground cinnamon

1/2 teaspoon vanilla extract

Pinch of salt

Cinnamon sugar for dusting (optional)

Nutritional Information (Per Serving): Calories: 120| Total Fat: 2g| Saturated Fat: 0.5g| Cholesterol: 5mg| Protein: 7g| Sodium: 30mg| Carbohydrates: 20g| Dietary Fiber: 1g| Sugar: 15g

Hints and Tactics

For added crunch, sprinkle crushed snicker doodle cookies on top before serving. Try make use of a drizzle of caramel sauce for indulgence.

Direction

1. In the Ninja Creami blending pitcher, combine almond milk, maple syrup (or agave syrup), vanilla protein powder, ground cinnamon, vanilla extract, and a pinch of salt.
2. Secure the blending pitcher onto the Ninja Creami base and blend on medium speed until the mixture is well-combined.
3. Pour the mixture into the Ninja Creami freezing container.
4. Attach the whipping accessory and set the Ninja Creami to "Sorbet" mode.
5. Once the sorbet reaches a creamy consistency, transfer it to an airtight container and freeze for an additional 24 hours to firm up.
6. Serve the Snicker doodle Protein Sorbet in bowls, optionally dusted with cinnamon sugar for an extra touch.

Embark on a flavorful journey with the Protein Beetroot Orange Ginger Sorbet, a unique blend that combines the earthiness of beetroot with the zesty kick of orange and the warmth of ginger. This protein-rich sorbet is a refreshing and health-conscious choice.

Prep Time: 10 minutes| Churning Time: 15 minutes| Freezing Time: 24 hours| Serves: 4 servings

Ingredients

1 cup beetroot juice

1/2 cup orange juice

1/4 cup honey or agave syrup

1 scoop vanilla protein powder

1 teaspoon fresh ginger, grated

Zest of 1 orange

Pinch of salt

Nutritional Information (Per Serving): Calories: 110| Total Fat: 1g| Saturated Fat: 0.5g| Cholesterol: 5mg| Protein: 6g| Sodium: 30mg| Carbohydrates: 25g| Dietary Fiber: 2g| Sugar: 20g

Hints and Tactics

Add a dash of ground ginger to elevate the flavor. Try incorporating a hint of beetroot powder for a boost in color.

Direction

1. In the Ninja Creami blending pitcher, combine beetroot juice, orange juice, honey (or agave syrup), vanilla protein powder, grated fresh ginger, orange zest, and a pinch of salt.
2. Secure the blending pitcher onto the Ninja Creami base and blend on medium speed until the mixture is well-combined.
3. Pour the mixture into the Ninja Creami freezing container.
4. Attach the whipping accessory and set the Ninja Creami to "Sorbet" mode.
5. Once the sorbet reaches a creamy consistency, transfer it to an airtight container and freeze for an additional 24 hours to firm up.
6. Serve the Protein Beetroot Orange Ginger Sorbet in bowls or cones for a unique and nutritious experience.

Easy Passion Protein Sorbet

Experience the tropical allure with the Easy Passion Protein Sorbet, a simple and protein-packed treat that captures the exotic flavor of passion fruit. This easy-to-make sorbet is a delightful way to indulge in a taste of paradise.

Prep Time: 5 minutes| Churning Time: 15 minutes| Freezing Time: 18 hours| Serves: 4 servings

Ingredients

1 cup passion fruit puree

1/2 cup coconut water

1/4 cup honey or agave syrup

1 scoop vanilla protein powder

Zest of 1 lime

Pinch of salt

Fresh mint leaves for garnish (optional)

Nutritional Information (Per Serving): Calories: 120| Total Fat: 1g| Saturated Fat: 0.5g| Cholesterol: 5mg| Protein: 6g| Sodium: 30mg| Carbohydrates: 25g| Dietary Fiber: 2g| Sugar: 20g

Hints and Tactics

For an extra burst of freshness, add a squeeze of lime juice before freezing. Try experiment with adding diced mango for a tropical twist.

Direction

1. In the Ninja Creami blending pitcher, combine passion fruit puree, coconut water, honey (or agave syrup), vanilla protein powder, lime zest, and a pinch of salt.

2. Secure the blending pitcher onto the Ninja Creami base and blend on medium speed until the mixture is well-combined.

3. Pour the mixture into the Ninja Creami freezing container.

4. Attach the whipping accessory and set the Ninja Creami to "Sorbet" mode.

5. Once the sorbet reaches a creamy consistency, transfer it to an airtight container and freeze for an additional 18 hours to firm up.

6. Serve the Easy Passion Protein Sorbet in bowls or cones, garnished with fresh mint leaves if desired.

Enjoy the vibrant and sweet essence of apricots in a wholesome treat with the Apricot Protein Sorbet. This protein-packed sorbet is a refreshing way to savor the natural goodness of ripe apricots while staying nourished.

Prep Time: 10 minutes| Churning Time: 15 minutes| Freezing Time: 14 hours| Serves: 4 servings

Ingredients

2 cups ripe apricots, pitted and chopped

1/4 cup honey or agave syrup

1 scoop vanilla protein powder

1 tablespoon fresh lemon juice

Zest of 1 lemon

Pinch of salt

Fresh mint leaves for garnish (optional)

Nutritional Information (Per Serving): Calories: 130| Total Fat: 1g| Saturated Fat: 0.5g| Cholesterol: 5mg| Protein: 6g| Sodium: 30mg| Carbohydrates: 30g| Dietary Fiber: 3g| Sugar: 25g

Hints and Tactics

Before freezing, try folding in some sliced apricot pieces for some texture. Try adding a small pinch of ground ginger for an additional taste dimension.

Direction

1. In the Ninja Creami blending pitcher, combine chopped ripe apricots, honey (or agave syrup), vanilla protein powder, fresh lemon juice, lemon zest, and a pinch of salt.

2. Secure the blending pitcher onto the Ninja Creami base and blend on medium speed until the mixture is well-combined.

3. Pour the mixture into the Ninja Creami freezing container.

4. Attach the whipping accessory and set the Ninja Creami to "Sorbet" mode.

5. Once the sorbet reaches a creamy consistency, transfer it to an airtight container and freeze for an additional 14 hours to firm up.

6. Serve the Apricot Protein Sorbet in bowls or cones, garnished with fresh mint leaves if desired.

Savor the natural sweetness of fresh figs in a delightful and protein-packed treat with the Simple Fresh Protein Fig Sorbet. This easy-to-make sorbet captures the essence of ripe figs, offering a refreshing and nutritious way to indulge your taste buds.

Prep Time: 10 minutes| Churning Time: 15 minutes| Freezing Time: 24 hours| Serves: 4 servings

Ingredients

2 cups fresh figs, stemmed and quartered

1/4 cup honey or agave syrup

1 scoop vanilla protein powder

1 tablespoon fresh lemon juice

Zest of 1 lemon

Pinch of salt

Chopped pistachios for garnish (optional)

Nutritional Information (Per Serving): Calories: 120| Total Fat: 1g| Saturated Fat: 0.5g| Cholesterol: 5mg| Protein: 6g| Sodium: 30mg| Carbohydrates: 30g| Dietary Fiber: 4g| Sugar: 25g

Hints and Tactics

❖ Before serving, think about adding a little drizzle of balsamic glaze for an additional layer of flavor.

❖ Try adding a tiny bit of cinnamon for a cozy, fragrant touch.

Direction

1. In the Ninja Creami blending pitcher, combine quartered fresh figs, honey (or agave syrup), vanilla protein powder, fresh lemon juice, lemon zest, and a pinch of salt.

2. Secure the blending pitcher onto the Ninja Creami base and blend on medium speed until the mixture is well-combined.

3. Pour the mixture into the Ninja Creami freezing container.

4. Attach the whipping accessory and set the Ninja Creami to "Sorbet" mode.

5. Once the sorbet reaches a creamy consistency, transfer it to an airtight container and freeze for an additional 24 hours to firm up.

6. Serve the Simple Fresh Protein Fig Sorbet in bowls, optionally garnished with chopped pistachios for added texture.

Verbena Sorbet

Refresh your palate with the vibrant and tangy flavors of Verbena Sorbet. This light and fruity sorbet offer a delightful combination of citrusy notes, making it a perfect palate cleanser or a refreshing dessert on a warm day.

Prep Time: 15 minutes| Chilling Time: 18 hours| Serves: 4 servings

Ingredients

1 cup fresh verbena leaves (lemon verbena)

1 cup water

1 cup granulated sugar

1/4 cup fresh lemon juice

Zest of 1 lemon

Nutritional Information (Per Serving): Calories: 120| Total Fat: 0g| Saturated Fat: 0g| Cholesterol: 0mg| Protein: 1g| Sodium: 5mg| Carbohydrates: 30g| Dietary Fiber: 0g| Sugar: 28g

Hints and Tactics

Explore different citrus notes such as lime or orange to create a vibrant citrus blend. Enhance the presentation with a garnish of a fresh verbena sprig or a twist of orange zest.

Direction

1. In a saucepan, combine fresh verbena leaves, water, and granulated sugar. Heat to a low simmer, stirring to dissolve the sugar. Remove from heat.
2. Allow the verbena-infused syrup to cool to room temperature.
3. Strain the syrup to remove the verbena leaves, leaving a smooth liquid.
4. In a mixing bowl, combine the verbena-infused syrup with fresh lemon juice and lemon zest.
5. Pour the mixture into the Ninja Creami freezing container.
6. Attach the whipping accessory and set the Ninja Creami to "Sorbet" mode.
7. Once the sorbet reaches a creamy consistency, transfer it to an airtight container and freeze for an additional 18 hours to firm up.
8. Serve the Verbena Sorbet in bowls or cones for a zesty and refreshing treat.

Vanilla Bean Gelato

Savor the timeless elegance of Vanilla Bean Gelato, a classic frozen treat enriched with the aromatic essence of real vanilla beans. This luscious and creamy gelato is a delightful indulgence that showcases the purity and simplicity of quality ingredients

Prep Time: 15 minutes| Churning Time: 20 minutes| Freezing Time: 18 hours| Serves: 4 servings

Ingredients

2 cups whole milk

1/2 cup granulated sugar

1 tablespoon pure vanilla extract

2 vanilla beans, split and seeds scraped

1/4 teaspoon salt

Nutritional Information (Per Serving): Calories: 200| Total Fat: 8g| Saturated Fat: 5g| Cholesterol: 25mg| Protein: 5g| Sodium: 60mg| Carbohydrates: 30g| Dietary Fiber: 0g| Sugar: 28g

Hints and Tactics

Try varying the varieties of vanilla beans to achieve subtle variations in flavor. For a fun twist, top with some fresh berries or a caramel drizzle.

Direction

1. In a saucepan, heat whole milk and granulated sugar over medium heat until the sugar dissolves. Allow it to cool.
2. Add the scraped vanilla bean seeds and split vanilla beans to the milk mixture.
3. Cover and let the mixture infuse for at least 30 minutes to allow the vanilla flavor to develop.
4. Remove the vanilla beans and discard them. The infused milk should now carry the rich aroma of vanilla.
5. In the Ninja Creami blending pitcher, combine the vanilla-infused milk, pure vanilla extract, and a pinch of salt.
6. Pour the mixture into the Ninja Creami freezing container.
7. Attach the whipping accessory and set the Ninja Creami to "Gelato" mode.
8. Once the gelato reaches a creamy consistency, transfer it to an airtight container and freeze for an additional 18 hours to firm up.
9. Serve the Vanilla Bean Gelato in bowls or cones for a pure and indulgent experience.

Indulge in the triple delight of rich chocolate flavor, creamy texture, and a protein-packed punch with the Triple Protein Chocolate Gelato. This decadent frozen treat combines the goodness of three protein sources to create a luscious and guilt-free chocolate experience

Prep Time: 15 minutes| Churning Time: 20 minutes| Freezing Time: 24 hours| Serves: 4 servings

Ingredients

2 cups whole milk

1/2 cup granulated sugar

1/3 cup unsweetened cocoa powder

1 scoop chocolate whey protein powder

1 scoop chocolate plant-based protein powder

1 scoop chocolate casein protein powder

1 teaspoon vanilla extract

Pinch of salt

Nutritional Information (Per Serving): Calories: 220| Total Fat: 6g| Saturated Fat: 4g| Cholesterol: 20mg| Protein: 15g| Sodium: 70mg| Carbohydrates: 30g| Dietary Fiber: 3g| Sugar: 25g

Hints and Tactics

In the final minutes of churning, think about adding a handful of chunks of dark chocolate for even more richness. Try out various protein powder combinations to achieve a range of nutritional profiles

Direction

1. In a saucepan, heat whole milk and granulated sugar over medium heat until the sugar dissolves. Allow it to cool.

2. In the Ninja Creami blending pitcher, combine the cooled milk mixture, unsweetened cocoa powder, chocolate whey protein powder, chocolate plant-based protein powder, chocolate casein protein powder, vanilla extract, and a pinch of salt.

3. Pour the mixture into the Ninja Creami freezing container.

4. Attach the whipping accessory and set the Ninja Creami to "Gelato" mode.

5. Once the gelato reaches a creamy consistency, transfer it to an airtight container and freeze for an additional 24 hours to firm up.

6. Serve the Triple Protein Chocolate Gelato in bowls or cones for a chocolate lover's dream with the added benefits of triple protein goodness.

Indulge your chocolate cravings with the Sweet Dark Chocolate Sorbet, a decadent and dairy-free treat that brings together the richness of dark chocolate with a touch of sweetness. This sorbet is a luscious and guilt-free way to satisfy your love for chocolate.

Prep Time: 10 minutes| Churning Time: 15 minutes| Freezing Time: 24 hours| Serves: 4 servings

Ingredients

1 cup dark chocolate (70% cocoa or higher), chopped

1/2 cup coconut milk

1/4 cup maple syrup or agave syrup

1/2 teaspoon vanilla extract

Pinch of salt

Fresh berries for garnish (optional)

Nutritional Information (Per Serving): Calories: 180| Total Fat: 12g| Saturated Fat: 8g| Cholesterol: 0mg| Protein: 2g| Sodium: 10mg| Carbohydrates: 20g| Dietary Fiber: 3g| Sugar: 15g

Hints and Tactics

For added texture, fold in chopped nuts or chocolate chunks before freezing.
Experiment with a sprinkle of sea salt for a delightful contrast.

Direction

1. Use a microwave or double boiler to melt the dark chocolate in a heatproof bowl. Allow it to cool slightly.

2. In the Ninja Creami blending pitcher, combine melted dark chocolate, coconut milk, maple syrup (or agave syrup), vanilla extract, and a pinch of salt.

3. Secure the blending pitcher onto the Ninja Creami base and blend on medium speed until the mixture is well-combined.

4. Pour the mixture into the Ninja Creami freezing container.

5. Attach the whipping accessory and set the Ninja Creami to "Sorbet" mode.

6. Once the sorbet reaches a creamy consistency, transfer it to an airtight container and freeze for an additional 24 hours to firm up.

7. Serve the Sweet Dark Chocolate Sorbet in bowls, garnished with fresh berries if desired.

Protein-Packed Chocolate Avocado Mousse

Indulge in the velvety richness of Protein-Packed Chocolate Avocado Mousse, a guilt-free dessert that combines the creaminess of avocado with the decadence of chocolate. This protein-enriched treat is a delicious way to satisfy your sweet tooth while promoting a healthy lifestyle.

Prep Time: 15 minutes| Chilling Time: 2 hours| Serves: 4 servings

Ingredients

2 ripe avocados, peeled and pitted

1/2 cup unsweetened cocoa powder

1/4 cup honey or agave syrup

1 scoop chocolate protein powder

1 teaspoon vanilla extract

Pinch of salt

Fresh berries for garnish (optional)

Nutritional Information (Per Serving): Calories: 180| Total Fat: 12g| Saturated Fat: 2g| Cholesterol: 0mg| Protein: 6g| Sodium: 10mg| Carbohydrates: 20g| Dietary Fiber: 8g| Sugar: 8g

Hints and Tactics

For added texture, sprinkle chopped nuts or shredded coconut on top.

Experiment with a dash of cinnamon for a subtle spice.

Direction

1. In a food processor or blender, combine ripe avocados, cocoa powder, honey (or agave syrup), chocolate protein powder, vanilla extract, and a pinch of salt.

2. Blend the ingredients prior to the mixture is smooth and creamy.

3. Divide the mousse into serving glasses or bowls.

4. Chill the mousse in the refrigerator for at least 2 hours to allow it to set.

5. If desired, garnish with fresh berries prior to serving.

Red Velvet Protein Delight Gelato

Enjoy the opulent and very protein-rich Red Velvet Protein Delight Gelato. With an added protein boost, this rich and velvety delicacy perfectly embodies the flavors of red velvet cake and offers a guilt-free way to sate your sweet tooth.

Prep Time: 15 minutes| Churning Time: 20 minutes| Freezing Time: 18 hours| Serves: 4 servings

Ingredients

2 cups whole milk

1/2 cup granulated sugar

1 scoop chocolate protein powder

1 tablespoon unsweetened cocoa powder

1 teaspoon vanilla extract

Red food coloring (as desired)

Cream cheese frosting swirl (optional)

Nutritional Information (Per Serving): Calories: 220| Total Fat: 6g| Saturated Fat: 3.5g| Cholesterol: 20mg| Protein: 8g| Sodium: 70mg| Carbohydrates: 35g| Dietary Fiber: 1g| Sugar: 30g

Hints and Tactics

Enhance the texture by incorporating crushed red velvet cookies before placing it in the freezer. Explore an extra layer of indulgence by experimenting with a generous drizzle of chocolate sauce.

Direction

1. In a saucepan, heat whole milk and granulated sugar over medium heat until the sugar dissolves. Allow it to cool.

2. In the Ninja Creami blending pitcher, combine the cooled milk mixture, chocolate protein powder, cocoa powder, vanilla extract, and red food coloring. Blend until well-combined.

3. Pour the mixture into the Ninja Creami freezing container.

4. Attach the whipping accessory and set the Ninja Creami to "Gelato" mode.

5. Once the gelato reaches a creamy consistency, add a swirl of cream cheese frosting if desired. Transfer to an airtight container and freeze for an additional 18 hours to firm up.

6. Serve the Red Velvet Protein Delight Gelato in bowls or cones for a decadent and protein-enriched treat.

Elevate your dessert experience with the Espresso Toffee Protein Temptation Gelato. This protein-rich indulgence combines the bold flavors of espresso and the sweet crunch of toffee for a sophisticated and tempting treat.

Prep Time: 15 minutes| Churning Time: 20 minutes| Freezing Time: 6 hours| Serves:| 4 servings

Ingredients

2 cups whole milk

1/2 cup granulated sugar

1 scoop vanilla protein powder

2 tablespoons instant espresso powder

1/4 cup toffee bits

1 teaspoon vanilla extract

Nutritional Information (Per Serving):| Calories: 200| Total Fat: 6g| Saturated Fat: 3.5g| Cholesterol: 20mg| Protein: 7g| Sodium: 50mg| Carbohydrates: 30g| Dietary Fiber: 0g| Sugar: 25g

Hints and Tactics

Before serving, add more toffee bits on top for an added crunch. Try adding a caramel drizzle for a rich, luscious garnish.

Direction

1. In a saucepan, heat whole milk and granulated sugar over medium heat until the sugar dissolves. Allow it to cool.

2. In the Ninja Creami blending pitcher, combine the cooled milk mixture, vanilla protein powder, instant espresso powder, toffee bits, and vanilla extract. Blend until well-combined.

3. Pour the mixture into the Ninja Creami freezing container.

4. Attach the whipping accessory and set the Ninja Creami to "Gelato" mode.

5. Once the gelato reaches a creamy consistency, transfer it to an airtight container and freeze for an additional 4 hours to firm up.

6. Serve the Espresso Toffee Protein Temptation Gelato in bowls or cones for a coffee-infused and protein-enriched dessert.

Delight in the decadent and protein-packed goodness of Brownie Batter Protein Extravaganza Gelato. This indulgent treat captures the rich flavors of brownie batter, offering a guilt-free way to satisfy your chocolate cravings while boosting your protein intake.

Prep Time: 15 minutes| Churning Time: 20 minutes| Freezing Time: 4 hours| Serves: 4 servings

Ingredients

2 cups whole milk

1/2 cup granulated sugar

1 scoop chocolate protein powder

1/4 cup unsweetened cocoa powder

1/2 cup brownie batter chunks

1 teaspoon vanilla extract

Nutritional Information (Per Serving): Calories: 230| Total Fat: 7g| Saturated Fat: 4g| Cholesterol: 25mg| Protein: 9g| Sodium: 60mg| Carbohydrates: 35g| Dietary Fiber: 2g| Sugar: 30g

Hints and Tactics

Before serving, pour melted chocolate over the gelato for an added delight. Try adding a little amount of chopped nuts for texture.

Direction

1. In a saucepan, heat whole milk and granulated sugar over medium heat until the sugar dissolves. Allow it to cool.

2. In the Ninja Creami blending pitcher, combine the cooled milk mixture, chocolate protein powder, cocoa powder, brownie batter chunks, and vanilla extract. Blend until well-combined.

3. Pour the mixture into the Ninja Creami freezing container.

4. Attach the whipping accessory and set the Ninja Creami to "Gelato" mode.

5. Once the gelato reaches a creamy consistency, transfer it to an airtight container and freeze for an additional 4 hours to firm up.

6. Serve the Brownie Batter Protein Extravaganza Gelato in bowls or cones for a chocolate lover's dream with added protein goodness.

Experience sophistication in every bite with White Chocolate Pistachio Protein Elegance Gelato. This protein-rich treat combines the creamy sweetness of white chocolate with the nutty crunch of pistachios, offering an elegant and delightful dessert.

Prep Time: 15 minutes| Churning Time: 20 minutes| Freezing Time: 4 hours| Serves: 4 servings

Ingredients

2 cups whole milk

1/2 cup granulated sugar

1 scoop vanilla protein powder

1/2 cup white chocolate chips

1/4 cup chopped pistachios

1 teaspoon vanilla extract

Nutritional Information (Per Serving):| Calories: 210| Total Fat: 8g| Saturated Fat: 4g| Cholesterol: 20mg| Protein: 7g| Sodium: 50mg| Carbohydrates: 30g| Dietary Fiber: 1g| Sugar: 25g

Hints and Tactics

For added elegance, top with a sprinkle of edible gold flakes before serving. Experiment with a drizzle of honey for a touch of sophistication.

Direction

1. In a saucepan, heat whole milk and granulated sugar over medium heat until the sugar dissolves. Allow it to cool.
2. In the Ninja Creami blending pitcher, combine the cooled milk mixture, vanilla protein powder, white chocolate chips, chopped pistachios, and vanilla extract. Blend until well-combined.
3. Pour the mixture into the Ninja Creami freezing container.
4. Attach the whipping accessory and set the Ninja Creami to "Gelato" mode.
5. Once the gelato reaches a creamy consistency, transfer it to an airtight container and freeze for an additional 4 hours to firm up.
6. Serve the White Chocolate Pistachio Protein Elegance Gelato in bowls or cones for a refined and protein-enriched dessert experience.

Fior di Latte Gelato

Experience sophistication in every bite with White Chocolate Pistachio Protein Elegance Gelato. This protein-rich treat combines the creamy sweetness of white chocolate with the nutty crunch of pistachios, offering an elegant and delightful dessert.

Prep Time: 15 minutes| Churning Time: 20 minutes| Freezing Time: 4 hours| Serves: 4 servings

Ingredients

2 cups whole milk

1 cup heavy cream

3/4 cup granulated sugar

1 teaspoon vanilla extract

Pinch of salt

Nutritional Information (Per Serving): Calories: 280, Total Fat: 18g Saturated Fat: 12g Cholesterol: 60mg Protein: 5g Sodium: 50mg Carbohydrates: 26g Dietary Fiber: 0g Sugar: 25g

Hints and Tactics

Enhance the creaminess by adding an extra tablespoon of heavy cream if desired. For a touch of elegance, consider garnishing with a sprinkle of powdered sugar.

Direction

1. Mix heavy cream and full milk in a saucepan. Heat until it gently simmers over medium heat. Remove from heat.
2. In a mixing bowl, whisk together granulated sugar, vanilla extract, and a pinch of salt.
3. Gradually pour the hot milk and cream mixture into the sugar mixture, stirring continuously until the sugar dissolves.
4. Let the mixture cool until it reaches room temperature.
5. Pour the Fior di Latte mixture into the Ninja Creami freezing container.
6. Attach the whipping accessory and set the Ninja Creami to "Gelato" mode.
7. Once the gelato reaches a creamy consistency, transfer it to an airtight container and freeze for an additional 4 hours to firm up.
8. Serve the Fior di Late Gelato in bowls or cones for a taste of pure milk bliss.

Acknowledgments

As I pen down the final pages of the "Healthy Ninja Creami Protein Cookbook," I am filled with immense gratitude for the incredible individuals who have played an instrumental role in bringing this culinary journey to fruition.

A heartfelt thank you to the team at Ninja for crafting an innovative kitchen companion in the Ninja Creamy. Your dedication to excellence and commitment to empowering home cooks have truly enriched the culinary landscape.

A special thank you to the talented chefs and nutrition experts who shared their expertise, insights, and passion for protein-based cooking. Your guidance has not only elevated the recipes but has also contributed to the educational aspect of this cookbook, fostering a deeper understanding of protein-rich culinary practices.

I extend my appreciation to the broader community of home cooks and food enthusiasts who shared their enthusiasm for protein-based creations. Your creativity and passion for healthy, delicious meals have inspired me throughout this endeavor.

Special thanks to the online culinary community, where the exchange of ideas and shared experiences fostered an atmosphere of continuous learning and growth.

Last but certainly not least, a profound thank you to you, the reader. Your interest in the "Healthy Ninja Creami Protein Cookbook" is the ultimate reward. May these recipes bring joy and nourishment to your kitchen.

With sincere gratitude,

Caroline

Caroline Eve, RDN

Protein-Packed 7 Day Meal Plan

	BREAKFAST	SNACKS	LUNCH	DINNER
DAY 1	**Spirulina Smoothie Sunshine** • Protein: Spirulina is a protein-rich superfood. • Nutrient Focus: Iron and other essential nutrients from spirulina.	**Mocha Protein Affogato** • Protein: Coffee and protein powder for a pick-me-up. • Nutrient Focus: Caffeine for alertness.	**Cucumber Cooler** • Protein: Moderate protein from yogurt. • Nutrient Focus: Hydration and cooling effect.	**Caramel Fudge Protein Indulgence Ice Cream** • Protein: Indulgent treat with protein. • Nutrient Focus: Satisfying sweet cravings.
DAY 2	**Tropical Sunrise Bow** • Protein: Moderate plant-based protein. • Nutrient Focus: Vitamin C from tropical fruits.	**Greek Yogurt Berry Parfait with Protein Granola** • Protein: Greek yogurt and protein granola for sustained energy.	**Broccoli Bliss Smoothie** • Protein: Plant-based protein from broccoli. • Nutrient Focus: Fiber and essential nutrients from broccoli.	**Blackberry Protein Burst Ice Cream** • Protein: Blackberry provides antioxidants, and the protein supports muscle recovery.
DAY 3	**Strawberry Protein Blast Ice Cream** • Protein: Strawberry delight with protein. • Nutrient Focus: Vitamin C from strawberries.	**Spiced Latte Protein Shake** • Protein: Coffee and protein combo. • Nutrient Focus: Warm and comforting.	**Blueberry Muffin Blast** • Protein: Blueberries and protein for a satisfying meal.	**Chocolate Avocado Protein Shake** • Protein: Creamy shake with healthy fats from avocado
DAY 4	**Pineapple Protein Tropical Swirl Ice Cream** • Protein: Pineapple and protein for a tropical start.	**Vanilla Berry Protein Shake** • Protein: Berry and protein goodness. • Nutrient Focus: Antioxidants from berries.	**Coconut Protein Colada Shake** • Protein: Coconut milk and protein powder. • Nutrient Focus: Healthy fats from coconut.	**Raspberry Ripple Protein Delight Ice Cream** • Protein: Raspberry goodness with added protein
DAY 5	**Chocolate Protein Power Ice Cream** • Protein: Start your day with a chocolaty protein-packed ice cream delight. • Nutrient Focus: Enjoy the antioxidant properties of chocolate.	**Fior di Latte Gelato** • Protein: Creamy and rich gelato experience.	**Protein-Packed Chocolate Avocado Mousse** • Protein: Decadent mousse with healthy fats from avocado.	**White Chocolate Pistachio Protein Elegance Gelato** • Protein: Luxurious gelato with the goodness of pistachios
DAY 6	**Golden Milk Smoothie** • Protein: Turmeric-infused smoothie with protein. • Nutrient Focus: Anti-inflammatory properties of turmeric	**Shamrock Shake** • Protein: A refreshing shake with a hint of mint. • Nutrient Focus: Refreshing and energizing.	**Dragon Fruit Delight Smoothie** • Protein: Dragon fruit goodness with added protein.	**Red Velvet Protein Delight Gelato** • Protein: Decadent gelato with the allure of red velvet.
DAY 7	**Papaya Passion Protein Sorbet** • Protein: Refreshing sorbet with a tropical twist.	**Kahlua Mocha Milkshake** • Protein: A mocha-infused milkshake with a touch of indulgence. • Nutrient Focus: Caffeine for a midday boost.	**Cherry Chocolate Protein Fusion Ice Cream** • Protein: A fusion of cherry and chocolate with the benefits of added protein.	**Superb Brownie Batter Protein Bowl Gelato** • Protein: Satisfy your sweet tooth with a bowl of brownie batter gelato rich in protein.

Additional Tips

- Stay hydrated throughout the day by drinking plenty of water.
- Adjust portion sizes based on individual dietary goals and energy needs.
- Incorporate a variety of fruits and vegetables for a diverse range of nutrients.
- Engage in regular physical activity to support overall well-being.

Shopping List

Proteins:
- Chicken breast (boneless, skinless)
- Greek yogurt
- Protein powder (vanilla, chocolate)
- Eggs

Dairy:
- Milk (coconut, almond)
- Vanilla almond milk
- Greek yogurt
- Whipping cream

Ice Cream/Gelato Ingredients:
- Dark chocolate chunks
- Cocoa powder
- Toffee bits

Fruits
- Pineapple
- Banana
- Mango
- Peach
- Lemon
- Blackberry
- Strawberry
- Raspberry
- Blueberry
- Papaya
- Fig

Others:
- Tortilla chips (for smoothie bowls)
- Dark chocolate chips (optional)

Vegetables:
- Broccoli
- Cucumber
- Avocado

Nuts and Seeds:
- Shredded coconut (unsweetened)
- Pistachios

Herbs and Spices:
- Spirulina
- Turmeric
- Cinnamon
- Vanilla extract

Bakery:
- Granola (protein-rich)
- Whole grain oats
- Flour (all-purpose)

Beverages:
- Coffee beans (or ground coffee)
- Tea (chai)
- Coconut water

Frozen:
- Frozen pineapple chunks
- Frozen mixed berries

Sweeteners:
- Honey or agave syrup

NINJA CREAMI RECIPE TRACKER

Recipe Title

Date:

Ingredients:

INGREDIENTS	QUANLITY	NOTE

Base Recipes:
- Used Frozen Base Choose One): [ ]Vanilla Yogurt [ ] Banana Ice Cream [ ] Protein Powder Mix [ ] Other:--------
- Additional Liquid (If Needed)_____
- Adjustmrnt (Spices, Extract, etc.):_____

Ninja Creami Settings:
- Churn Time_____
- Re-Spin: Yes/No (if yes, how many times) _____:

Texture
- Smooth & Creamy [ ]
- Slightly Icy [ ]
- Chunky [ ]

- Prep Time: _____ minutes
- Cooking/Freezing Time: _____ minutes/hours
- Serving Size: _____ people
- Nutritional Information (Per Serving):

Overall Rating: 1-5 Stars

REMARKS

Recipes Title:

Date:

Ingredients:

INGREDIENTS	QUANLITY	NOTE

Base Recipes:
- Used Frozen Base Choose One): [ ]Vanilla Yogurt [ ] Banana Ice Cream [ ] Protein Powder Mix [ ] Other:--------
- Additional Liquid (If Needed)_____
- Adjustmrnt (Spices, Extract, etc.):_____

Ninja Creami Settings:
- Churn Time_____
- Re-Spin: Yes/No (if yes, how many times) _____:

Texture
- Smooth & Creamy [ ]
- Slightly Icy [ ]
- Chunky [ ]

- Prep Time: _____ minutes
- Cooking/Freezing Time: _____ minutes/hours
- Serving Size: _____ people
- Nutritional Information (Per Serving):

Overall Rating: 1-5 Stars

REMARKS

NINJA CREAMI RECIPE TRACKER

Recipe Title

Date:

Ingredients:

INGREDIENTS	QUANLITY	NOTE

Base Recipes:
- Used Frozen Base Choose One): [ ]Vanilla Yogurt [ ] Banana Ice Cream [ ] Protein Powder Mix [ ] Other:--------
- Additional Liquid (If Needed)_____
- Adjustmrnt (Spices, Extract, etc.):_____

Ninja Creami Settings:
- Churn Time_____
- Re-Spin: Yes/No (if yes, how many times) _____:

Texture
- Smooth & Creamy   [ ]
- Slightly Icy   [ ]
- Chunky   [ ]

- Prep Time: _____ minutes
- Cooking/Freezing Time: _____ minutes/hours
- Serving Size: _____ people
- Nutritional Information (Per Serving):

Overall Rating: 1-5 Stars

REMARKS

Recipes Title:

Date:

Ingredients:

INGREDIENTS	QUANLITY	NOTE

Base Recipes:
- Used Frozen Base Choose One): [ ]Vanilla Yogurt [ ] Banana Ice Cream [ ] Protein Powder Mix [ ] Other:--------
- Additional Liquid (If Needed)_____
- Adjustmrnt (Spices, Extract, etc.):_____

Ninja Creami Settings:
- Churn Time_____
- Re-Spin: Yes/No (if yes, how many times) _____:

Texture
- Smooth & Creamy   [ ]
- Slightly Icy   [ ]
- Chunky   [ ]

- Prep Time: _____ minutes
- Cooking/Freezing Time: _____ minutes/hours
- Serving Size: _____ people
- Nutritional Information (Per Serving):

Overall Rating: 1-5 Stars

REMARKS

NINJA CREAMI RECIPE TRACKER

Recipe Title

Date:

Ingredients:

INGREDIENTS	QUANLITY	NOTE

Base Recipes:
- Used Frozen Base Choose One): [ ]Vanilla Yogurt [ ] Banana Ice Cream [ ] Protein Powder Mix [ ] Other:--------
- Additional Liquid (If Needed)_____
- Adjustmrnt (Spices, Extract, etc.):_____

Ninja Creami Settings:
- Churn Time_____
- Re-Spin: Yes/No (if yes, how many times) _____:

Texture
- Smooth & Creamy   [ ]
- Slightly Icy   [ ]
- Chunky   [ ]

- Prep Time: _____ minutes
- Cooking/Freezing Time: _____ minutes/hours
- Serving Size: _____ people
- Nutritional Information (Per Serving):

Overall Rating: 1-5 Stars

REMARKS

Recipes Title:

Date:

Ingredients:

INGREDIENTS	QUANLITY	NOTE

Base Recipes:
- Used Frozen Base Choose One): [ ]Vanilla Yogurt [ ] Banana Ice Cream [ ] Protein Powder Mix [ ] Other:--------
- Additional Liquid (If Needed)_____
- Adjustmrnt (Spices, Extract, etc.):_____

Ninja Creami Settings:
- Churn Time_____
- Re-Spin: Yes/No (if yes, how many times) _____:

Texture
- Smooth & Creamy   [ ]
- Slightly Icy   [ ]
- Chunky   [ ]

- Prep Time: _____ minutes
- Cooking/Freezing Time: _____ minutes/hours
- Serving Size: _____ people
- Nutritional Information (Per Serving):

Overall Rating: 1-5 Stars

REMARKS

NINJA CREAMI RECIPE TRACKER

Recipe Title

Date:

Ingredients:

INGREDIENTS	QUANLITY	NOTE

Base Recipes:
- Used Frozen Base Choose One): [ ]Vanilla Yogurt [ ] Banana Ice Cream [ ] Protein Powder Mix [ ] Other:--------
- Additional Liquid (If Needed)_____
- Adjustmrnt (Spices, Extract, etc.):_____

Ninja Creami Settings:
- Churn Time_____
- Re-Spin: Yes/No (if yes, how many times) _____:

Texture
- Smooth & Creamy   [ ]
- Slightly Icy   [ ]
- Chunky   [ ]

- Prep Time: _____ minutes
- Cooking/Freezing Time: _____ minutes/hours
- Serving Size: _____ people
- Nutritional Information (Per Serving):

Overall Rating: 1-5 Stars [★ ★ ★ ★ ★]

REMARKS

Recipes Title:

Date:

Ingredients:

INGREDIENTS	QUANLITY	NOTE

Base Recipes:
- Used Frozen Base Choose One): [ ]Vanilla Yogurt [ ] Banana Ice Cream [ ] Protein Powder Mix [ ] Other:--------
- Additional Liquid (If Needed)_____
- Adjustmrnt (Spices, Extract, etc.):_____

Ninja Creami Settings:
- Churn Time_____
- Re-Spin: Yes/No (if yes, how many times) _____:

Texture
- Smooth & Creamy   [ ]
- Slightly Icy   [ ]
- Chunky   [ ]

- Prep Time: _____ minutes
- Cooking/Freezing Time: _____ minutes/hours
- Serving Size: _____ people
- Nutritional Information (Per Serving):

Overall Rating: 1-5 Stars [★ ★ ★ ★ ★]

REMARKS

NINJA CREAMI RECIPE TRACKER

Recipe Title

Date:

Ingredients:

INGREDIENTS	QUANLITY	NOTE

Base Recipes:

- Used Frozen Base Choose One): [ ]Vanilla Yogurt [ ] Banana Ice Cream [ ] Protein Powder Mix [ ] Other:--------
- Additional Liquid (If Needed)_____
- Adjustmrnt (Spices, Extract, etc.):_____

Ninja Creami Settings:

- Churn Time_____
- Re-Spin: Yes/No (if yes, how many times) _____:

Texture

- Smooth & Creamy   [ ]
- Slightly Icy   [ ]
- Chunky   [ ]

- Prep Time: _____ minutes
- Cooking/Freezing Time: _____ minutes/hours
- Serving Size: _____ people
- Nutritional Information (Per Serving):

Overall Rating: 1-5 Stars ⭐⭐⭐⭐⭐

REMARKS

Recipes Title:

Date:

Ingredients:

INGREDIENTS	QUANLITY	NOTE

Base Recipes:

- Used Frozen Base Choose One): [ ]Vanilla Yogurt [ ] Banana Ice Cream [ ] Protein Powder Mix [ ] Other:--------
- Additional Liquid (If Needed)_____
- Adjustmrnt (Spices, Extract, etc.):_____

Ninja Creami Settings:

- Churn Time_____
- Re-Spin: Yes/No (if yes, how many times) _____:

Texture

- Smooth & Creamy   [ ]
- Slightly Icy   [ ]
- Chunky   [ ]

- Prep Time: _____ minutes
- Cooking/Freezing Time: _____ minutes/hours
- Serving Size: _____ people
- Nutritional Information (Per Serving):

Overall Rating: 1-5 Stars ⭐⭐⭐⭐⭐

REMARKS

NINJA CREAMI RECIPE TRACKER

Recipe Title

Date:

Ingredients:

INGREDIENTS	QUANLITY	NOTE

Base Recipes:

- Used Frozen Base Choose One): [ ]Vanilla Yogurt [ ] Banana Ice Cream [ ] Protein Powder Mix [ ] Other:--------
- Additional Liquid (If Needed)_____
- Adjustmrnt (Spices, Extract, etc.):_____

Ninja Creami Settings:

- Churn Time_____
- Re-Spin: Yes/No (if yes, how many times) _____:

Texture

- Smooth & Creamy   [ ]
- Slightly Icy   [ ]
- Chunky   [ ]

- Prep Time: _____ minutes
- Cooking/Freezing Time: _____ minutes/hours
- Serving Size: _____ people
- Nutritional Information (Per Serving):

Overall Rating: 1-5 Stars

REMARKS

Recipes Title:

Date:

Ingredients:

INGREDIENTS	QUANLITY	NOTE

Base Recipes:

- Used Frozen Base Choose One): [ ]Vanilla Yogurt [ ] Banana Ice Cream [ ] Protein Powder Mix [ ] Other:--------
- Additional Liquid (If Needed)_____
- Adjustmrnt (Spices, Extract, etc.):_____

Ninja Creami Settings:

- Churn Time_____
- Re-Spin: Yes/No (if yes, how many times) _____:

Texture

- Smooth & Creamy   [ ]
- Slightly Icy   [ ]
- Chunky   [ ]

- Prep Time: _____ minutes
- Cooking/Freezing Time: _____ minutes/hours
- Serving Size: _____ people
- Nutritional Information (Per Serving):

Overall Rating: 1-5 Stars

REMARKS

NINJA CREAMI RECIPE TRACKER

Recipe Title

Date:

Ingredients:

INGREDIENTS	QUANLITY	NOTE

Base Recipes:
- Used Frozen Base Choose One): [ ]Vanilla Yogurt [ ] Banana Ice Cream [ ] Protein Powder Mix [ ] Other:--------
- Additional Liquid (If Needed)_____
- Adjustmrnt (Spices, Extract, etc.):_____

Ninja Creami Settings:
- Churn Time_____
- Re-Spin: Yes/No (if yes, how many times) _____:

Texture
- Smooth & Creamy [ ]
- Slightly Icy [ ]
- Chunky [ ]

- Prep Time: _____ minutes
- Cooking/Freezing Time: _____ minutes/hours
- Serving Size: _____ people
- Nutritional Information (Per Serving):

Overall Rating: 1-5 Stars ★ ★ ★ ★ ★

REMARKS

Recipes Title:

Date:

Ingredients:

INGREDIENTS	QUANLITY	NOTE

Base Recipes:
- Used Frozen Base Choose One): [ ]Vanilla Yogurt [ ] Banana Ice Cream [ ] Protein Powder Mix [ ] Other:--------
- Additional Liquid (If Needed)_____
- Adjustmrnt (Spices, Extract, etc.):_____

Ninja Creami Settings:
- Churn Time_____
- Re-Spin: Yes/No (if yes, how many times) _____:

Texture
- Smooth & Creamy [ ]
- Slightly Icy [ ]
- Chunky [ ]

- Prep Time: _____ minutes
- Cooking/Freezing Time: _____ minutes/hours
- Serving Size: _____ people
- Nutritional Information (Per Serving):

Overall Rating: 1-5 Stars ★ ★ ★ ★ ★

REMARKS

NINJA CREAMI RECIPE TRACKER

Recipe Title

Date:

Ingredients:

INGREDIENTS	QUANLITY	NOTE

Base Recipes:
- Used Frozen Base Choose One): [ ]Vanilla Yogurt [ ] Banana Ice Cream [ ] Protein Powder Mix [ ] Other:--------
- Additional Liquid (If Needed)_____
- Adjustmrnt (Spices, Extract, etc.):_____

Ninja Creami Settings:
- Churn Time_____
- Re-Spin: Yes/No (if yes, how many times) _____:

Texture
- Smooth & Creamy   [ ]
- Slightly Icy   [ ]
- Chunky   [ ]

- Prep Time: _____ minutes
- Cooking/Freezing Time: _____ minutes/hours
- Serving Size: _____, people
- Nutritional Information (Per Serving):

Overall Rating: 1-5 Stars ⬤⬤⬤⬤⬤

REMARKS

Recipes Title:

Date:

Ingredients:

INGREDIENTS	QUANLITY	NOTE

Base Recipes:
- Used Frozen Base Choose One): [ ]Vanilla Yogurt [ ] Banana Ice Cream [ ] Protein Powder Mix [ ] Other:--------
- Additional Liquid (If Needed)_____
- Adjustmrnt (Spices, Extract, etc.):_____

Ninja Creami Settings:
- Churn Time_____
- Re-Spin: Yes/No (if yes, how many times) _____:

Texture
- Smooth & Creamy   [ ]
- Slightly Icy   [ ]
- Chunky   [ ]

- Prep Time: _____ minutes
- Cooking/Freezing Time: _____ minutes/hours
- Serving Size: _____ people
- Nutritional Information (Per Serving):

Overall Rating: 1-5 Stars ⬤⬤⬤⬤⬤

REMARKS

NINJA CREAMI RECIPE TRACKER

Recipe Title

Date:

Ingredients:

INGREDIENTS	QUANLITY	NOTE

Base Recipes:
- Used Frozen Base Choose One): [ ]Vanilla Yogurt [ ] Banana Ice Cream [ ] Protein Powder Mix [ ] Other:--------
- Additional Liquid (If Needed)_____
- Adjustmrnt (Spices, Extract, etc.):_____

Ninja Creami Settings:
- Churn Time_____
- Re-Spin: Yes/No (if yes, how many times) _____:

Texture
- Smooth & Creamy   [ ]
- Slightly Icy   [ ]
- Chunky   [ ]

- Prep Time: _____ minutes
- Cooking/Freezing Time: _____ minutes/hours
- Serving Size: _____ people
- Nutritional Information (Per Serving):

Overall Rating: 1-5 Stars

REMARKS

Recipes Title:

Date:

Ingredients:

INGREDIENTS	QUANLITY	NOTE

Base Recipes:
- Used Frozen Base Choose One): [ ]Vanilla Yogurt [ ] Banana Ice Cream [ ] Protein Powder Mix [ ] Other:--------
- Additional Liquid (If Needed)_____
- Adjustmrnt (Spices, Extract, etc.):_____

Ninja Creami Settings:
- Churn Time_____
- Re-Spin: Yes/No (if yes, how many times) _____:

Texture
- Smooth & Creamy   [ ]
- Slightly Icy   [ ]
- Chunky   [ ]

- Prep Time: _____ minutes
- Cooking/Freezing Time: _____ minutes/hours
- Serving Size: _____ people
- Nutritional Information (Per Serving):

Overall Rating: 1-5 Stars

REMARKS

NINJA CREAMI RECIPE TRACKER

Recipe Title

Date:

Ingredients:

INGREDIENTS	QUANLITY	NOTE

Base Recipes:
- Used Frozen Base Choose One): [ ]Vanilla Yogurt [ ] Banana Ice Cream [ ] Protein Powder Mix [ ] Other:--------
- Additional Liquid (If Needed)_____
- Adjustmrnt (Spices, Extract, etc.):_____

Ninja Creami Settings:
- Churn Time_____
- Re-Spin: Yes/No (if yes, how many times) _____:

Texture
- Smooth & Creamy   [ ]
- Slightly Icy   [ ]
- Chunky   [ ]

- Prep Time: _____ minutes
- Cooking/Freezing Time: _____ minutes/hours
- Serving Size: _____ people
- Nutritional Information (Per Serving):

Overall Rating: 1-5 Stars ⬤⬤⬤⬤⬤

REMARKS

Recipes Title:

Date:

Ingredients:

INGREDIENTS	QUANLITY	NOTE

Base Recipes:
- Used Frozen Base Choose One): [ ]Vanilla Yogurt [ ] Banana Ice Cream [ ] Protein Powder Mix [ ] Other:--------
- Additional Liquid (If Needed)_____
- Adjustmrnt (Spices, Extract, etc.):_____

Ninja Creami Settings:
- Churn Time_____
- Re-Spin: Yes/No (if yes, how many times) _____:

Texture
- Smooth & Creamy   [ ]
- Slightly Icy   [ ]
- Chunky   [ ]

- Prep Time: _____ minutes
- Cooking/Freezing Time: _____ minutes/hours
- Serving Size: _____ people
- Nutritional Information (Per Serving):

Overall Rating: 1-5 Stars ⬤⬤⬤⬤⬤

REMARKS

NINJA CREAMI RECIPE TRACKER

Recipe Title

Date:

Ingredients:

INGREDIENTS	QUANLITY	NOTE

Base Recipes:
- Used Frozen Base Choose One): [ ]Vanilla Yogurt [ ] Banana Ice Cream [ ] Protein Powder Mix [ ] Other:--------
- Additional Liquid (If Needed)_____
- Adjustmrnt (Spices, Extract, etc.):_____

Ninja Creami Settings:
- Churn Time_____
- Re-Spin: Yes/No (if yes, how many times) _____:

Texture
- Smooth & Creamy   [ ]
- Slightly Icy   [ ]
- Chunky   [ ]

- Prep Time: _____ minutes
- Cooking/Freezing Time: _____ minutes/hours
- Serving Size: _____ people
- Nutritional Information (Per Serving):

Overall Rating: 1-5 Stars ☆☆☆☆☆

REMARKS

Recipes Title:

Date:

Ingredients:

INGREDIENTS	QUANLITY	NOTE

Base Recipes:
- Used Frozen Base Choose One): [ ]Vanilla Yogurt [ ] Banana Ice Cream [ ] Protein Powder Mix [ ] Other:--------
- Additional Liquid (If Needed)_____
- Adjustmrnt (Spices, Extract, etc.):_____

Ninja Creami Settings:
- Churn Time_____
- Re-Spin: Yes/No (if yes, how many times) _____:

Texture
- Smooth & Creamy   [ ]
- Slightly Icy   [ ]
- Chunky   [ ]

- Prep Time: _____ minutes
- Cooking/Freezing Time: _____ minutes/hours
- Serving Size: _____ people
- Nutritional Information (Per Serving):

Overall Rating: 1-5 Stars ☆☆☆☆☆

REMARKS

VOLUME EQUIVALENT (DRY)

US Standard Measurement	Metric Equivalents
1/4 teaspoon	1.23 ml
1/2 teaspoon	2.46 ml
3/4 teaspoon	3.69 ml
1 teaspoon	4.93 ml
2 teaspoons	9.86 ml
1 tablespoon	14.79 ml
1/4 cup	59.15 ml
1/2 cup	118.3 ml
3/4 cup	177.45 ml
1 cup	236.6 ml
2 cups	473.2 ml
3 cups	709.8 ml
4 cups	946.4 ml

VOLUME EQUIVALENTS LIQUIDS

US Standard (Imperial)	Metric (SI)
1 fluid ounce (fl oz)	29.574 milliliters (ml)
1 cup	236.588 milliliters (ml)
1 pint (16 fl oz)	473.176 milliliters (ml)
1 quart (32 fl oz)	946.353 milliliters (ml)
1 gallon (128 fl oz)	3.785 liters (L)
1 tablespoon	14.787 milliliters (ml)
1 teaspoon	4.929 milliliters (ml)
1 milliliter (ml)	0.0338 fluid ounces (fl oz)
1 liter (L)	33.814 fluid ounces (fl oz)
1 liter (L)	1.0567 quarts
1 liter (L)	0.26417 gallons

TEMPERATURE EQUIVALENTS

Fahrenheit (°F)	Celsius (°C)
225 °F	107 °C
250 °F	120 °C
275 °F	135 °C
300 °F	150 °C
325 °F	160 °C
350 °F	180 °C
375 °F	190 °C
400 °F	205 °C
425 °F	220 °C
450 °F	235 °C
475 °F	245 °C
500 °F	260 °C

WEIGHT EQUIVALENTS

Ingredient	US Standard	Metric
1/2 ounce	14.175 grams	
1 ounce	28.35 grams	30 mL
2 ounces	60 grams	60 mL
5 ounces	150 grams	150 mL
10 ounces	300 grams	300 mL
16 ounces	450 grams	450 mL
1 pound	454 grams	454 mL
1.5 pounds	681 grams	681 mL
2 pounds	907 grams	907 mL

Apricot Protein Sorbet (66)

Autumn Glow Milkshake (54)

Banana Nut Protein Delight Ice Cream (35)

Blackberry Protein Burst Ice Cream (30)

Blueberry Muffin Blast (49)

Broccoli Bliss Smoothie (23)

Cantaloupe Protein Melon Sorbet (59)

Caramel Fudge Protein Indulgence Ice Cream (39)

Cherry Chocolate Protein Fusion Ice Cream (36)

Choco Cream Cheese Milkshake (55)

Chocolate Avocado Protein Shake (50)

Chocolate Gelato With The Triple Aim Protein (70)

Cinnamon Protein Chai Ice Cream (31)

Coffee Protein Punch Ice Cream (44)

Coconut Protein Colada Shake (47)

Coconut Protein Swirl Ice Cream (37)

Cream Protein And Cookies Happiness Ice Cream (41)

Cranberry Orange Protein Citrus Sorbet (62)

Cucumber Cooler (26)

Delicious Dark Chocolate Gelato (71)

Dragon Fruit Delight Smoothie (24)

Easy Passion Protein Sorbet (65)

Espresso Toffee Protein Temptation Gelato (74)

Fior Di Latte Gelato (77)

Golden Milk Smoothie (22)

Greek Yogurt Berry Parfait With Protein Granola (20)

Green Power Protein Smoothie (14)

Guava Sunrise Smoothie (25)

Honeydew Mint Protein Refresh Sorbet (60)

Kahlua Mocha Milkshake (53)

Lemon Protein Zest Ice Cream (34)

Mango Protein Tropical Temptation Ice Cream (38)

Mocha Protein Affogato (21)

Oatmeal Cookie Latte (48)

Orange Banana and Mango Shake (56

Papaya Passion Protein Sorbet (57)

Paradise Ice Cream With Peach Protein (33)

Paradise Ice Cream With Pistachio Protein (40)

Peanut Butter Cup Dream (32)

Pinktastic Pitaya Smoothie (16)

Pineapple Protein Tropical Swirl Ice Cream (27)

Pomegranate Protein Power Sorbet (58)

Protein Beetroot Orange Ginger Sorbet (64)

Protein-Packed Chocolate Avocado Mousse (72)

Raspberry Ripple Protein Delight Ice Cream (42)

Red Velvet Protein Delight Gelato (73)

Shamrock Shake (52)

Simple Fresh Protein Fig Sorbet (67)

Smoothie With Green Hulk (15)

Snickerdoodle Protein Sorbet (63)

Spirulina Smoothie Sunshine (18)

Strawberry Protein Blast Ice Cream (43)

Strawberry Shortcake Smoothie (19)

Superb Brownie Batter Protein Bowl Gelato (75)

Sweet Potato Pie Spice Protein Smoothie (17)

Tropical Sunrise Bowl (13)

Vanilla Almond Protein Swirl Ice Cream (29)

Vanilla Berry Protein Shake (46)

Verbena Sorbet (68)

White Chocolate Pistachio Protein Elegance Gelato (76)

Thanks for Reading!

Made in United States
Troutdale, OR
05/03/2024